GCSE OCR Gateway
Core Science
Higher Workbook

This book is for anyone doing **GCSE OCR Gateway Core Science** at higher level. It covers everything you'll need for your year 10 exams.

It's full of **tricky questions**... each one designed to make you **sweat** — because that's the only way you'll get any **better**.

There are questions to see **what facts** you know. There are questions to see how well you can **apply those facts**. And there are questions to see what you know about **how science works**.

It's also got some daft bits in to try and make the whole experience at least vaguely entertaining for you.

What CGP is all about

Our sole aim here at CGP is to produce the highest quality books — carefully written, immaculately presented and dangerously close to being funny.

Then we work our socks off to get them out to you — at the cheapest possible prices.

Contents

MODULE B2 — UNDERSTANDING OUR ENVIRONMENT

MODULE C2 — CHEMICAL RESOURCES

MODULE P2 — LIVING FOR THE FUTURE

Published by CGP

Editors:
Katie Braid, Emma Elder, Mary Falkner, Murray Hamilton, David Hickinson,
Edmund Robinson, Lyn Setchell, Hayley Thompson, Jane Towle and Dawn Wright.

Contributors:
Michael Aicken, Steve Coggins, Mark A Edwards, Rebecca Harvey, Frederick Langridge,
Claire Ruthven, Andy Rankin, Adrian Schmit, Sidney Stringer Community School,
Paul Warren, Jim Wilson and Chris Workman.

ISBN: 978 1 84146 714 6

With thanks to Helen Brace, Joe Brazier, Philip Dobson, Mark A Edwards, Judith Hayes,
Paul Jordin and David Ryan for the proofreading.

With thanks to Jan Greenway, Laura Jakubowski and Laura Stoney for the copyright research.

GORE-TEX®, GORE®, and designs are registered trademarks of W.L. Gore and Associates.
This book contains copyrighted material reproduced with the permission of
W.L. Gore and Associates. Copyright 2011 W.L. Gore and Associates.

Every effort has been made to locate copyright holders and obtain permission to reproduce
sources. For those sources where it has been difficult to trace the originator of the work,
we would be grateful for information. If any copyright holder would like us to make an
amendment to the acknowledgements, please notify us and we will gladly update the book
at the next reprint. Thank you.

Groovy website: www.cgpbooks.co.uk

Printed by Elanders Ltd, Newcastle upon Tyne.
Jolly bits of clipart from CorelDRAW®

Based on the classic CGP style created by Richard Parsons.

Preventing and Treating Infectious Disease

Q1   **Immunisation** involves injecting dead or inactive microorganisms into the body.

a) Tick the box to show whether the following statements about polio immunisation are **true** or **false**.

True False

i) The dead or inactive polio microorganisms have some of the same antigens as the live pathogen. ☐ ☐

ii) White blood cells produce antibodies against the antigens on the injected polio microorganisms. ☐ ☐

iii) After immunisation, memory cells can produce antibodies to fight infections of typhoid. ☐ ☐

iv) Immunisation is a type of passive immunity. ☐ ☐

b) Circle the correct words to complete the paragraph.

> In active immunity the immune system makes its own **antibodies / antigens**, but in
> passive immunity they come from **vaccination / another organism**. Active immunity
> is **permanent / temporary**, but passive immunity is **permanent / temporary**.

Q2 a) Give two **benefits** of immunisation.

1. ....

2. ....

b) Give **one** possible **risk** of immunisation.

....

Q3   John gets injected with the **rubella vaccine** but James doesn't. Soon afterwards both boys are exposed to the rubella virus. Explain in detail why James gets ill but John doesn't.

....

....

....

....

....

Preventing and Treating Infectious Disease

Q4 Tick the box to show whether the following statements are **true** or **false**.

True False

a) Antibiotics help bacteria to grow. ☐ ☐

b) MRSA is an example of an antibiotic-resistant strain of bacteria. ☐ ☐

c) Doctors overprescribing antibiotics has helped antibiotic-resistant bacteria to develop. ☐ ☐

Q5 Rachel has a **viral infection**, but when she visits her doctor he refuses to give her antibiotics.

a) Explain why her doctor is right.

....

....

b) What type of drug could her doctor prescribe?

....

Q6 The graph shows the number of **bacteria Y** in Gary's blood during a two-week course of **antibiotics**.

Symptoms are present when the level of bacteria is above this line.

a) How long after starting the course of antibiotics will Gary's symptoms disappear?

....

b) Why is it important for Gary to **finish** his full course of antibiotics?

....

....

Top Tips: Nobody really thought about all the problems that the misuse of antibiotics might cause until it was too late. Now we've got to come up with new ways to fight these antibiotic-resistant 'superbugs' — my suggestion of a microscopic rolled-up newspaper wasn't met with much approval.

Cancer and Drug Development

Q1   **Cancer** is caused by cells dividing out of control.

a)   Explain the difference between **benign** and **malignant** cancer tumours.

....

....

b)   Give two examples of changes people can make to their **lifestyle** or **diet** which might reduce their risk of getting cancer.

1. ....

2. ....

Q2   Write numbers in the boxes below to show the correct **order** in which drugs are tested.

◻ Drug is tested on human tissue

◻ Drug is tested on live animals

◻ Human volunteers are used to test the drug

◻ Computer models simulate a response to the drug

Q3   A pharmaceutical company is trialling a new drug. They are using a **placebo** in the trial and are conducting the trials 'double blind'.

a)   What is a placebo?

....

b)   Why are the scientists using a placebo?

....

....

c)   What is a double blind trial?

....

....

Drugs: Use and Harm

Q1 a) What is a **drug**?

....

b) Some people can become **addicted** to drugs. What does this mean?

....

....

c) Some drugs cause the body to develop a **tolerance** to them. What does this mean?

....

....

Q2 **Complete** the table below, which shows different types of drug and their effects on the body.

Type of drug	Example	Effects
Depressants		
	Paracetamol	Reduce the number of 'painful' stimuli at the nerve endings near an injury
Stimulants		Increase the activity of the brain
	Anabolic steroids	
		Distort what is seen and heard by altering the pathways that the brain sends messages along

Q3 Three people were arrested and charged with drug offences. Janice had been found taking ketamine (a class C drug). Paul and Duncan had been discovered taking amphetamines (a class B drug). Paul had obtained the drugs and had given some to Duncan.

a) Who is likely to receive the **most** severe punishment? Explain your answer.

....

....

b) Who is likely to receive the **least** severe punishment? Explain your answer.

....

....

Smoking and Alcohol

Q1 Smoking can cause a lot of different **health problems**.

a) Name **one** disease that can be caused by smoking.

....

b) Pregnant women are strongly advised not to smoke.
What effect can smoking have on a baby's birth weight?

....

Q2 **Alcohol** damages the cells in your body.

Describe the effect of excessive alcohol intake on the **liver**.

....

....

....

....

Q3 In the UK, the legal limit for alcohol in the blood when driving is
80 mg per 100 cm³. The table shows the number of 'units' of alcohol
in different drinks. One **unit** increases the blood alcohol level by
over **20 mg per 100 cm³** in most people.

DRINK	ALCOHOL UNITS
1 pint of strong lager	3
1 pint of beer	2
1 single measure of whisky	1

a) Bill drinks two pints of strong lager. How many units of alcohol has he had?

....

b) Is Bill's blood alcohol level likely to mean that he cannot legally drive? Explain your answer.

....

....

Assume he drank the pints fairly quickly.

c) Explain why it can be dangerous to drive a car after drinking alcohol.

....

Smoking and Alcohol

Q4   Tick the boxes next to the following statements to show whether they are **true** or **false**.

True False

a)   The main effect of alcohol is to increase the activity of the nervous system.   ☐ ☐

b)   People's coordination, balance and judgement improve when they drink alcohol.   ☐ ☐

c)   Alcohol causes dehydration, which can damage cells in the brain.   ☐ ☐

Q5   The graph shows how the number of **smokers** aged between 35 and 54 in the UK has changed since 1950.

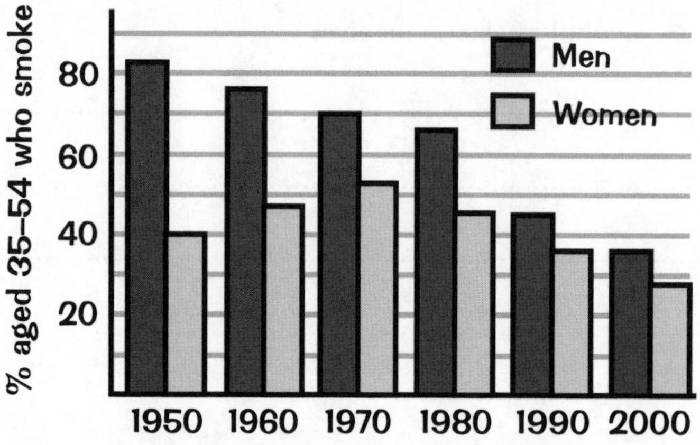

a)   What percentage of **men** smoked in 1970?

....

b)   Describe the main **trends** you can see in this graph.

....

....

....

....

c)   Explain how smoking causes **smoker's cough.**

....

....

....

___

Top Tips: The facts about what cigarettes and alcohol do to your body are pretty nasty and off-putting. It's good for you to know them, so you can choose a healthy lifestyle.

13

Receptors — The Eye

Q1   Write **labels** in the spaces to complete the diagram of a human eye.

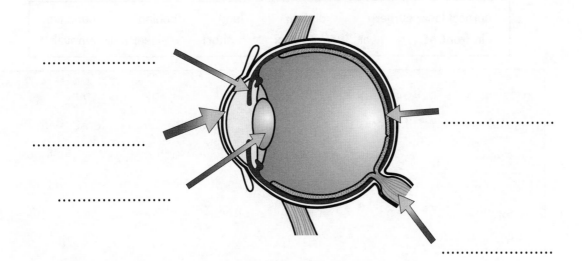

....

....

....

....

....

Q2   **Complete the table** about the functions of different parts of the eye.

Part of the eye	Function
....	Focuses light on the retina
....	Carries impulses from the eye to the brain
Retina	....
Ciliary muscles	....
....	Controls how much light enters the pupil

Q3   **Circle** the correct word in each pair to complete the passage below.

The eye focuses light by changing the shape of the **elastic / rigid lens**.

This is known as **accommodation / adaptation**.

When you look at distant objects, your ciliary muscle **contracts / relaxes**, and the

suspensory ligaments **tighten / slacken**. The lens becomes **more rounded / less rounded**

and light is refracted **more / less**. To focus on near objects the opposite actions happen.

<u>Receptors — The Eye</u>

Q4 Fill in the blanks in the paragraph using some of the words from the list below.

| corneal laser surgery | distant | long | behind | concave |
| in front of | near | convex | short | laser hair removal |

Long-sighted people can't focus on .... objects. This can be because their eyeball is too .... Glasses or contact lenses with a .... lens can correct this problem. Short-sighted people can't focus on .... objects. This problem can be caused by a person's eyeball being too .... , but it can be corrected by glasses or contact lenses with a .... lens. .... is an alternative to glasses and contact lenses to correct long- and short-sightedness.

Q5 The picture below shows a bird with **binocular vision**.

a) **Binocular vision** allows the bird to judge distances well. Explain how binocular vision works.

....

....

b) Give **one** disadvantage of binocular vision.

....

Q6 Gerald is **colour blind**. This means he has difficulty distinguishing between certain wavelengths of light.

a) Name the part of the eye that contains **light receptors**.

....

b) What is **red-green colour blindness** a result of?

....

Neurones and Reflexes

Q1 Circle the correct answer to complete each of the following sentences.

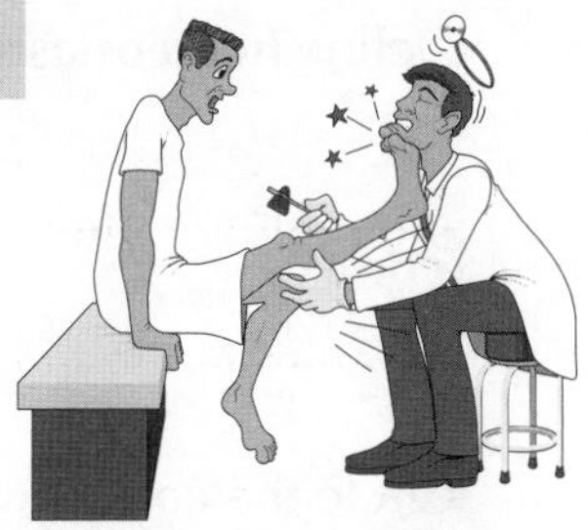

a) Reflexes happen **quickly** / **slowly**.

b) The main purpose of a reflex is to **protect** / **display** the body.

c) Reflexes happen **with** / **without** you thinking about them.

d) The pathway taken by a reflex is called a **reflex arc** / **reflex curve**.

Q2 Place numbers in the boxes to show the **passage of a reflex**, starting with 'stimulus'.

☐ Response   ☐ Sensory neurone   ☐ Receptor   ☐ Effector

☐ Motor neurone   [1] Stimulus   ☐ Relay neurone

Q3 The diagram below shows a typical **motor neurone**.

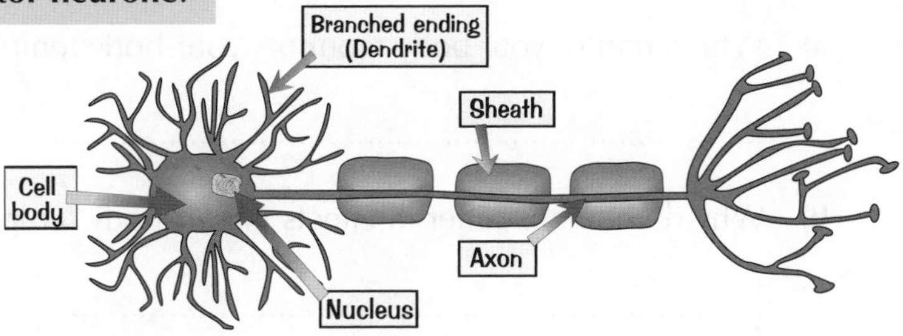

a) How does information travel along the neurone?

....

....

Branched ending (Dendrite), Sheath, Cell body, Axon, Nucleus

b) Why is it useful that the end of a neurone is **branched**?

....

c) What is the **function** of the sheath around the axon?

....

....

Q4 The gap between two neurones is called a **synapse**.

a) Explain how the information from a nerve impulse crosses the synapse.

....

b) Describe the effect of **stimulant** drugs on synapses.

....

....

Top Tips: Reflex actions are pretty useful. If your hand falls into a pan of boiling oil, you'll take your hand out **automatically**, rather than keeping it in there while you wonder what to do.

Module B1 — Understanding Ourselves

Homeostasis

Q1   Define **homeostasis**.

....

....

Q2   Circle the correct word in each pair to complete the passage below.

> Negative feedback is a response mechanism that **increases / counteracts** changes in
> the body's internal environment. For example, a rise in body temperature causes a
> response that **raises / lowers** body temperature. Negative feedback keeps the internal
> environment at an **optimum / upper** level at which cells can function properly.

Q3   The human body is usually maintained at a **temperature** of about **37 ºC**.

a)   Which part of your body monitors your body temperature to ensure that it is kept constant?

....

b)   Why do humans suffer ill effects if their body temperature varies too much from 37 °C?

....

....

c)   Name **one** condition you can get if you're exposed to:

i) high temperatures for a long time ....

ii) low temperatures for a long time ....

Q4   Your body has various techniques for adjusting body temperature to keep it constant.

a)   Explain how **sweating** helps to lower your body temperature.

....

....

b) i)   Explain what **vasodilation** and **vasoconstriction** are.

....

....

ii) How do vasodilation and vasoconstriction help to keep your body temperature constant?

....

....

Controlling Blood Sugar Level

Q1 Most people's **blood sugar** level is controlled by **homeostasis**.

a) Where does the **sugar** in your blood come from?

....

b) i) Name the **main hormone** involved in the regulation of blood sugar level.

....

ii) The hormone converts excess blood glucose into glycogen.
Name the **organ** where this takes place.

....

Q2 Complete the flow chart to show what happens when the **glucose** level in the blood gets too **high**.

> Blood contains too much glucose.

> .... is released
> by the ....

> .... makes the ....
> turn glucose into glycogen for storage.

> .... is removed
> from the ....

> Blood glucose level is now ....

Q3 Blood sugar level is controlled by a **hormone**.
Explain why nervous messages are faster than hormonal ones.

....

....

....

Controlling Blood Sugar Level

Q4   Ruby has **type 1 diabetes**.

a)   What is type 1 diabetes?

....

....

b)   Give two ways in which type 1 diabetics **control** their blood sugar level.

1. ....

2. ....

c)   Ruby injects insulin and then eats a meal.
Describe the effect of the insulin on her blood sugar level.

....

....

....

d)   Ruby starts playing hockey three times a week. Will this affect the insulin dosage she requires?
Explain your answer.

....

....

....

Q5   Paul has **type 2 diabetes**.

a)   What is type 2 diabetes?

....

....

b)   Describe how Paul can control his diabetes.

....

....

Top Tips: Although diabetes is a serious disease, many diabetics are able to control their blood sugar levels and carry on with normal lives. Sir Steve Redgrave even won a gold medal at the Olympics after he had been diagnosed with type 1 diabetes.

Module B1 — Understanding Ourselves

Plant Hormones and Growth

Q1   Tick the correct box to show whether the following statements are **true** or **false**.

True   False

a)   Plant shoots grow away from light.

b)   Plant roots grow towards light.

c)   Plant roots grow in the same direction that gravity acts.

d)   If the tip of a shoot is removed, the shoot may stop growing upwards.

Q2   Choose the correct word or phrase from each pair to complete the following paragraph.

> When a shoot tip is exposed to light from one side, auxin accumulates on the side that's in the **light / shade**. This makes the cells grow **faster / slower** on the shaded side, so the shoot bends **away from / towards** the light. This means that shoots are **positively / negatively** phototropic. When a root is exposed to light from one side, auxin accumulates on the side that's in the **light / shade**. This makes the cells grow **faster / slower** on the shaded side, so the root bends **towards / away from** the light. This means that roots are **positively / negatively** phototropic.

Q3   Two shoot tips were removed from young plants. Agar blocks soaked in **auxin** were placed on the cut ends of the shoots as shown in the diagram, and placed in the dark.

a)   Describe how auxin moves through a plant.

....

....

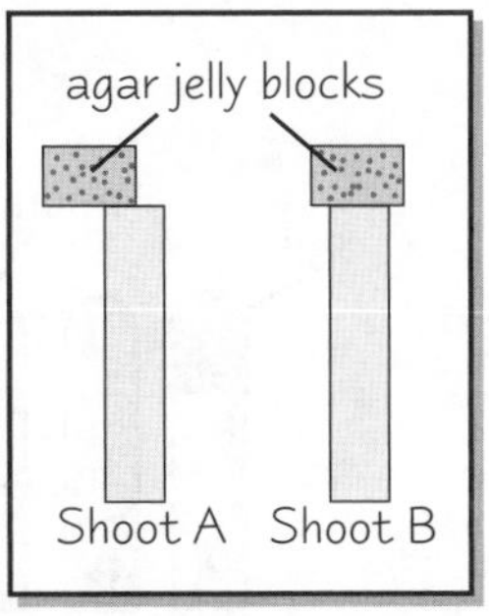

agar jelly blocks

Shoot A   Shoot B

b)   Describe the expected responses of shoots A and B to this treatment.

i) Shoot A ....

ii) Shoot B ....

c)   Explain your answers.

i) Shoot A ....

....

ii) Shoot B ....

....

Plant Hormones and Growth

Q4 Cedrick placed some **seedlings** on the surface of **damp soil** and left them for **five days**. The appearance of a seedling is shown in the diagram.

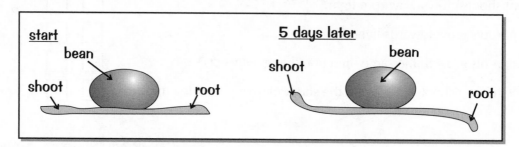

a) What **hormones** are responsible for these changes? ....

b) Where are these hormones produced? ....

c) Explain the responses of the shoot and the root to **gravity**.
For each one, say whether the response was **positively** or **negatively geotropic**.

   i) the shoot ....

   ....

   ii) the root ....

   ....

Q5 Vicky used three seedlings to investigate plant growth. Each seedling was prepared differently (see table). All three were placed in the same conditions, exposed to light from **one** direction and left for five hours. She recorded her results in the table below.

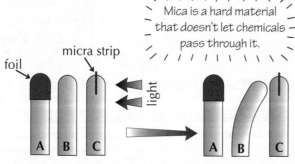

Seedling	Preparation	Observation after 5 hours
A	foil covering tip	no change
B	left alone	tip bent towards the light
C	mica strip through centre of tip	no change

Suggest why seedling A and seedling C failed to respond to the light.

Seedling A ....

....

Seedling C ....

....

Commercial Use of Plant Hormones

Q1 Describe four ways in which **plant hormones** can be used **commercially**.

1. ....

2. ....

3. ....

4. ....

Q2 Ronald owns a fruit farm which grows satsumas. The fruit is picked before it is ripe and transported to market.

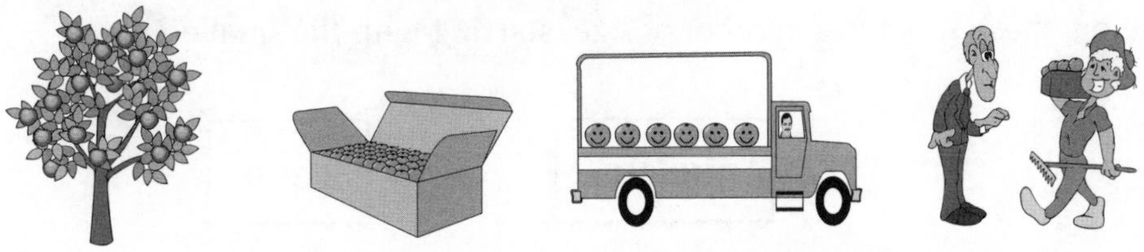

fruit picked ➩ fruit packaged ➩ fruit transported to market ➩ fruit displayed

a) Suggest why the satsumas are picked before they are ripe.

....

....

b) **i)** How could the unripened satsumas be ripened in time to reach the market?

....

ii) At what stage in the diagram above should the satsumas be ripened?

....

Q3 Charlie sprayed a batch of **dormant** barley seeds with a dilute solution of a plant hormone. This caused all the seeds to germinate.

a) Define the term **dormancy**.

....

b) Suggest **two** reasons why it is useful to be able to control when seeds germinate.

....

....

Genes and Chromosomes

Q1 Complete the passage by choosing from the words given below.
You can only use each word once.

| DNA | nucleus | gene |
| chromosomes | membrane | organ |

Almost every cell of the body is controlled by a structure called the ....

This structure contains strands of genetic material called ....

They are made of a chemical called .... Each section of genetic

material that controls a characteristic is called a ....

Q2 Write out these structures in order of size, **starting with the smallest.**

nucleus   gene

chromosome   cell

....

Q3 Tick the correct boxes to show whether each statement is **true** or **false**. **True False**

a) Human body cells contain 44 chromosomes. ☐ ☐

b) Chromosomes are long lengths of DNA. ☐ ☐

c) In most animal cells, chromosomes come in pairs. ☐ ☐

d) All species have the same number of chromosomes. ☐ ☐

Q4 Which of the following is the correct definition of the term **'alleles'**? Underline your choice.

'Alleles' is the collective term for all the genes found on a pair of chromosomes.

'Alleles' are different forms of the same gene.

'Alleles' are identical organisms produced by asexual reproduction.

___

Top Tips: You need to know exactly what's meant by genes, alleles, DNA, chromosomes, etc.
Once you understand all that, you'll be ready to get your head around the rest of this genetics malarkey.

Genetic Variation

Q1 Complete the table by putting a tick in the correct box. The first one has been done for you.

	Can cause variation	Does not cause variation
Formation of gametes from reproductive cells	✓	
Mutation of a reproductive cell		
Random fertilisation		
Conditions in the womb when the baby is developing		
Environmental effects after birth		

Q2 **One** of the statements below is **true**. Tick the box next to the correct one.

1. Neither your genes nor your environment are important in determining any of your attributes. ☐

2. Your health is only determined by your genes. ☐

3. Your environment is the most important factor for your sporting ability. ☐

4. It's hard to say if your genes or your environment are more important for characteristics like intelligence. ☐

Q3 The formation of gametes and fertilisation both cause **genetic variation**.

a) **i)** What are gametes? ....

ii) Explain how the formation of gametes results in genetic variation.

....

....

b) Explain how fertilisation causes genetic variation.

....

....

c) Most human body cells have **46** chromosomes. Explain why gametes need to have **23** chromosomes..

....

....

Genetic Diagrams

Q1 a) Are both versions of an allele always expressed?

....

b) When looking at a genetic diagram, how can you tell which is the dominant allele and which is the recessive allele?

....

....

c) An organism with two of the same alleles for a characteristic is known as what?

....

Q2 A type of fly usually has **red** eyes. However, there are a small number of white-eyed flies. Having **white** eyes is a **recessive** characteristic.

a) Complete the following sentences with either '**red eyes**' or '**white eyes**'.

i) R is the allele for ....

ii) r is the allele for ....

iii) Flies with alleles **RR** or **Rr** will have ....

iv) Flies with the alleles **rr** will have ....

b) Two flies have the alleles **Rr**. They fall in love and get it on.

i) Complete this genetic diagram to show the alleles of the possible offspring. One's been done for you.

parent's alleles

	R	r
R	RR	
r		

parent's alleles

ii) What is the probability that any one of the flies' offspring will have white eyes?

....

iii) The flies have 96 offspring. How many of the offspring are **likely** to have **red eyes**?

....

Genetic Diagrams

Q3 Draw lines to match each word to its **definition**.

| Genotype | | The characteristics expressed by an organism. |

| Phenotype | | The genetic makeup of an organism. |

Q4 An allele for the colour grey (**G**) in mice is dominant over the allele for the colour white (**g**). A heterozygous grey mouse (**Gg**) was bred with a homozygous white mouse (**gg**).

a) Complete the genetic diagram below to show the potential combinations of alleles in the offspring of the two mice.

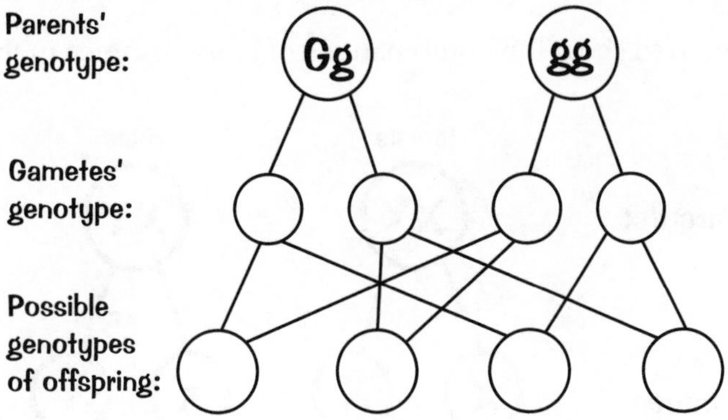

Parents' genotype: **Gg**   **gg**

Gametes' genotype:

Possible genotypes of offspring:

b) What is the likely ratio of colours in any offspring (grey : white)?

....

c) If the mice had 12 babies, how many would there most **likely** be of each colour?

....

Q5 Sally is investigating the inheritance of **flower colours**. She knows that the allele for the colour **red** is **dominant** and the allele for the colour **white** is **recessive**.

Sally has two of the same plant, one with **red** flowers and one with **white** flowers. Suggest how Sally can find out whether the red-flowered plant is homozygous red (**RR**) or heterozygous red (**Rr**).

....

....

....

....

....

Sex Inheritance and Genetic Disorders

Q1 Tick the boxes to show whether each statement is **true** or **false**.

	True	False

a) Women have two X chromosomes. Men have an X and a Y chromosome. ☐ ☐

b) There is a 75% chance that a couple's first child will be a girl. ☐ ☐

c) Sperm cells (male gametes) can carry an X or a Y chromosome. ☐ ☐

d) If the first born is a girl, the second born will always be a boy. ☐ ☐

Q2 Here is a genetic diagram showing the inheritance of **sex chromosomes** in humans.

a) Complete the diagram to show the combinations of chromosomes in the offspring.

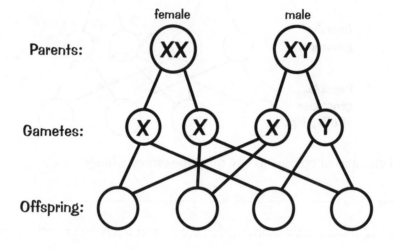

b) A woman becomes pregnant. What is the probability that the embryo is **male**?

....

c) Sarah says, "If I have eight children, four of them will definitely be boys."
Is Sarah right? Explain your answer.

....

....

....

Top Tips: The way the X and Y chromosomes are passed on is a nifty way of ensuring roughly equal numbers of men and women are born. Pretty useful for the survival of the species, I'd say.

Sex Inheritance and Genetic Disorders

Q3   **Cystic fibrosis** is a genetic (inherited) disorder that is caused by a **recessive allele**.

a)   How many copies of the allele do you need to be:

Carriers of genetic disorders don't show symptoms.

i)   a **carrier** of cystic fibrosis?

....

ii)   a **suffer** of cystic fibrosis?

....

b)   Complete the following genetic diagram showing the inheritance of cystic fibrosis.

Parents' genotype: **Ff**   **Ff**

Gametes' genotype:

Possible genotypes of offspring:

c)   i)   In the above genetic diagram, what is the probability of a child having cystic fibrosis?

....

ii)   In the above genetic diagram, what is the probability of a child being a **carrier** of the cystic fibrosis allele (but not having the disease)?

....

Q4   Sarah and Ahmad are expecting a baby. Tests have revealed that there is a **high chance** the baby will have a **genetic disorder** that could result in death within its first year of life. They have to decide whether to terminate the pregnancy.

a)   Give **one** argument that could be used in **favour** of a termination of the pregnancy.

....

....

b)   Give **one** argument that could be used **against** a termination of the pregnancy.

....

....

Mixed Questions — Module B1

Q1 **Protein** is one of six nutrients that help your body to function properly.

a) What are proteins made from? Circle the correct answer from the choice of words below.

amino acids   glycerol   fatty acids   proteases

b) Where are proteins stored in the body?

....

c) What condition is likely to develop in people whose diets don't have enough protein?

....

d) Explain the difference between the EAR of protein for a woman who is breast feeding and a woman who is not breast feeding.

....

....

Q2 Josephine has a **cold**. She has been researching colds on the internet and she has read that they are caused by **viruses**. Josephine has also read about an experimental drug that could be used to fight off infections like colds.

a) Could an **antibiotic** be used to clear up Josephine's cold? Explain your answer.

....

b) The experimental drug that Josephine read about is currently being tested on animals. It is due to be tested in a blind trial in a few months.

i) Suggest one way that the drug might have been tested before being tested on animals.

....

ii) Suggest one reason why people might object to animal testing.

....

iii) What is a blind trial?

....

....

> **Top Tips:** These mixed questions are kind of like the questions you'll get in your exam — each one could cover a variety of topics from the whole module, just to keep you on your toes...

Mixed Questions — Module B1

Q3 The diagram below shows how the **blood sugar level** is controlled in humans.

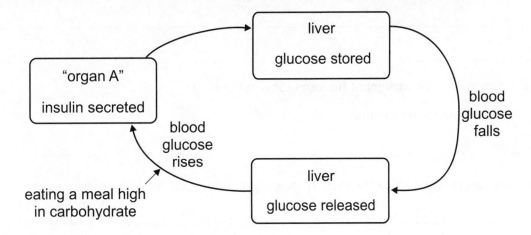

a) Name '**organ A**' in the diagram above.

....

b) Complete the following sentence:

Excess glucose is removed from your blood and stored in the liver as ....

c) Explain how the diagram shows an example of **negative feedback**.

....

....

Q4 Some people are **red-green colour blind** — this means that they can't tell the difference between red and green objects.

a) Tick the box next to the statement that is **true**.

1. Red-green colour blindness results from having too many cone cells in the retina. ☐

2. Red-green colour blindness results from a lack of specialised cone cells in the retina. ☐

3. Red-green colour blindness results from a problem with the optic nerve. ☐

4. Red-green colour blindness results from the lens being the wrong shape. ☐

b) Red-green colour blindness is caused by a recessive allele.

i) What are alleles?

....

ii) When are the characteristics of a recessive allele expressed?

....

Mixed Questions — Module B1

Q5 a) Suggest why smokers are more likely to suffer from **lung cancer** than non-smokers.

....

....

b) Lung cancer is when **malignant tumours** form in the lungs.

i) What is a malignant tumour?

....

ii) How can people reduce their risk of developing lung cancer?

....

Q6 Albinism is a genetic condition. Affected people, called albinos, lack any skin pigmentation. A couple, neither of whom is albino, have a child who is an albino.

Is the allele for albinism **dominant** or **recessive**? Explain your answer.

....

....

Q7 Sex determination in chickens is different from in humans. Male chickens (cockerels) have two Z chromosomes and females (hens) have ZW chromosomes.

a) Apart from having different letters, explain how this differs from human sex determination.

....

....

b) Complete the genetic diagram to show how sex is determined in chickens.

Parents: cockerel   hen

Chromosomes: (ZZ)   (ZW)

Gametes:

Chromosomes of offspring:

You don't need to know anything about chickens to answer this question — just apply what you already know about sex determination in humans.

c) What is the probability of any one fertilised chicken's egg developing into a cockerel?

....

Atoms, Molecules and Compounds

Q1 Say whether each of the following refers to the **nucleus** or the **electrons** within an atom.

a) Has a negative charge. .... **b)** Found at the centre of an atom. ....

c) Has a positive charge. .... **d)** Involved in chemical bonding. ....

Q2 **True** or **false?**

	True	False
a) In ionic bonding, ions lose or gain electrons to give atoms.	☐	☐
b) Ions with opposite charges attract each other.	☐	☐
c) Elements that lose electrons form positive ions.	☐	☐
d) Covalent bonding involves sharing electrons.	☐	☐

Q3 Complete the table showing the **names**, **displayed formulas**, **molecular formulas** and the number of **covalent bonds** for three carbon compounds.

NAME	DISPLAYED FORMULA	MOLECULAR FORMULA	NUMBER OF COVALENT BONDS
a)	H | H—C—H | H	**b)**	**c)**
ETHANE	H H | | H—C—C—H | | H H	**d)**	**e)**
PROPANE	H H H | | | H—C—C—C—H | | | H H H	**f)**	**g)**

Q4 The **displayed** formula for **ethanol** is shown on the right.

a) What is the molecular formula of ethanol? ....

b) How many atoms does a molecule of ethanol contain?

....

$$H-\underset{\underset{H}{|}}{\overset{\overset{H}{|}}{C}}-\underset{\underset{H}{|}}{\overset{\overset{H}{|}}{C}}-O-H$$

Q5 **Chemical formulas** are used to show elements and compounds.

a) What are the chemical formulas of the following elements and chompounds?

i) oxygen gas .... **ii)** carbon dioxide .... **iii)** sulfuric acid ....

b) State how many oxygen atoms there are in the following compounds.

i) H_2O .... **ii)** Na_2CO_3 .... **iii)** CO ....

Chemical Equations

Q1 This **equation** shows the formation of **carbon dioxide** when carbon is burned in air:

$$C + O_2 \rightarrow CO_2$$

a) Name the **reactant(s)** in this equation.

....

b) Name the **product(s)** in this equation.

....

c) How can you tell the equation is **balanced**?

....

Q2 Here is the equation for the production of **carbon monoxide** from a poorly ventilated charcoal flame. It is **not** balanced correctly.

$$C + O_2 \rightarrow CO$$

Circle the **correctly balanced** version of this equation.

$C + O_2 \rightarrow CO_2$

$C + O_2 \rightarrow 2CO$

$2C + O_2 \rightarrow 2CO$

Q3 A book describes a reaction as follows: "**Methane** (CH_4) burns in **oxygen** (O_2) to form **carbon dioxide** (CO_2) and **water** (H_2O)."

a) What are the **reactants** and the **products** in this reaction?

Reactants: .... Products: ....

b) Write the **word equation** for this reaction.

....

c) Write the **balanced symbol equation** for the reaction.

....

Don't forget — the oxygen ends up in both products.

Top Tips: The most important thing to remember with balancing equations is that you can't change the **little numbers** — if you do that then you'll change the substance into something completely different. Just take your time and work through everything logically.

Chemical Equations

Q4 **Lithium** reacts with **water** to produce **lithium hydroxide** (LiOH) and **hydrogen**.

a) Write the word equation for this reaction.

....

b) Write the balanced symbol equation for this reaction.

....

Q5 This unbalanced equation shows **magnesium chloride** being made from **magnesium carbonate**.

$$MgCO_3 + HCl \rightarrow MgCl_2 + H_2O + CO_2$$

a) Write the word equation for this reaction.

....

b) Write the balanced symbol equation for this reaction.

....

Q6 Add **one** number to each of these equations so that they are **correctly balanced**.

a) .... CuO + ... HBr → .... CuBr$_2$ + ... H$_2$O

b) .... H$_2$ + ... Br$_2$ → .... HBr

c) .... NaOH + ... H$_2$SO$_4$ → .... Na$_2$SO$_4$ + ... H$_2$O

I've left spaces in front of all the molecules so I don't give the game away. If a molecule doesn't need a number in front, just leave it blank.

Q7 **Balance** these equations.

a) .... NaOH + ... AlBr$_3$ → .... NaBr + ... Al(OH)$_3$

b) .... Fe + ... O$_2$ → .... Fe$_2$O$_3$

c) .... H−C−H (with H above and below) + ... Cl−Cl → .... Cl−C−Cl (with Cl above and below) + ... H−H

d) .... MgO + ... HNO$_3$ → .... Mg(NO$_3$)$_2$ + ... H$_2$O

e) .... CuSO$_4$ + ... NaOH → .... Cu(OH)$_2$ + ... Na$_2$SO$_4$

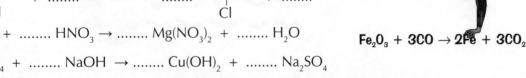
$Fe_2O_3 + 3CO \rightarrow 2Fe + 3CO_2$

Q8 Write the symbol equation for the reaction of **sodium carbonate** with **sulfuric acid**. The products of the reaction are **carbon dioxide**, **water** and **sodium sulfate** (Na$_2$SO$_4$).

....

Top Tip: Balancing equations is a simple matter of **trial and error** — keep changing one thing at a time until eventually you get the same number of each atom on both sides.

Emulsifiers

Q1 Imran is investigating the effects of different food additives on a mixture of **olive oil** and **water**. He sets up four flasks containing equal volumes of oil and water. He adds nothing else to the first one, and equal volumes of either **additive A**, **B** or **C** to the others. Then he gives them all a good shake and leaves them on a windowsill. After five days he notes their appearance in this table.

Additive used	Appearance after 5 days
None	Oil floating on water. Unpleasant smell.
A	Oil floating on water. No smell.
B	Oil floating on water. Unpleasant smell.
C	Oil and water mixed. Unpleasant smell.

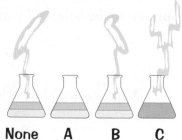

None A B C

a) Antioxidants are additives that prevent foods 'going off' as quickly, by preventing them from reacting with oxygen. Which one of the additives is:

  i) An antioxidant? ....

  ii) An emulsifier? ....

b) Justify your answers to part **a)**.

  i) ....

  ii) ....

c) Why does Imran set up a flask with no additives added?

  ....

d) Name a food that often contains an emulsifier. ....

Q2 **Lecithin** is added to chocolate drinks in order to prevent the oils separating out from the water. The diagram shows a molecule of lecithin.

a) Label the **hydrophilic** part and the **hydrophobic** part of the lecithin molecule.

b) Briefly explain how this molecule stops the oil and water parts of chocolate drinks from separating into two different layers.

  ....

  ....

  ....

Cooking and Chemical Change

Q1   When meat or eggs are cooked the **protein** molecules they contain are **denatured**.

Gas mark 7, licence to grill

a)   Explain how cooking causes this chemical change to proteins.

....

....

....

b)   Why does denaturing proteins in meat and eggs make them more appealing to eat?

....

c)   Is denaturing a protein a reversible change or an irreversible change? ....

Q2   Fill in the blanks in the passage using some of the words in the list below.

protein   cellulose   heat   starch   digest   swallow   water

> Potatoes are a good source of carbohydrate. Each potato cell is surrounded by
>
> a .... cell wall, which humans can't ....
>
> When the potato is cooked, the .... breaks down the cell wall.
>
> Cooking also makes the grains of .... inside the cells swell up.

Q3   **Baking powder** contains sodium hydrogen carbonate, $NaHCO_3$, which breaks down when heated.

a)   What is this type of chemical reaction called? ....

b) i)   Name the gas that's released. ....

ii)   Describe a chemical test for the gas released.

....

....

c)   Write a **word equation** for the breakdown of sodium hydrogen carbonate.

....

d)   Write the **balanced symbol equation** for this reaction.

....

Perfumes

Q1   New perfumes are sometimes tested on **animals**.

a)   Give one reason **for** testing cosmetic products on animals.

....

b)   Explain why testing of cosmetic products on animals is **banned** in the EU.

....

....

Q2   A fruity smelling ester can be made by reacting **ethanol** with **ethanoic acid**.

a)   Write a word equation for the **general** reaction used to make an ester.

....

b)   Write numbers in the boxes to put the instructions into the right order for making this ester.

☐   Warm the flask gently on an electric heating plate for 10 minutes.

☐   Put 15 cm^3 of ethanoic acid into a 100 cm^3 conical flask.

☐   When the flask is cool enough to handle, pour its contents into a 250 cm^3 beaker containing 100 cm^3 of sodium carbonate solution.

☐   Add 15 cm^3 of ethanol and a few drops of concentrated sulfuric acid.

☐   Turn off the heat.

c)   Suggest which of the above steps is carried out to speed up the reaction.

....

d)   What is the purpose of the sodium carbonate solution?

....

Q3   A chemist was asked by an **aftershave company** to make some new scents. Her new compounds were then **tested** to see if they were suitable for use in aftershaves. The results of the tests are summarised in the table on the right.

Scent	Does it evaporate easily?	Does it dissolve in water?	Does it react with water?
A	yes	no	yes
B	yes	yes	no
C	yes	no	no
D	no	no	no

a)   Which one of these would you use as the scent in an aftershave and why?

....

....

b)   Suggest a further test that should be carried out before the chemical can be used in the aftershave.

....

Module C1 — Carbon Chemistry

Kinetic Theory and Forces Between Particles

Q1   For each description below, say whether it refers to the particles of a **solid**, a **liquid** or a **gas**.

a)   There are virtually no forces between particles.   ....

b)   The particles can vibrate but cannot move from place to place.   ....

c)   The particles can move around but tend to stick together.   ....

d)   There are strong forces holding the particles together.   ....

e)   The particles move freely in straight lines.   ....

f)   There is no fixed volume or shape.   ....

g)   There is a fixed volume, but no fixed shape.   ....

Q2   Choose from the words in the list to fill in the blanks in this paragraph.

"We wanna be free to do what we wanna do."

speeds	moving	quickly	boiling
evaporation	slowly	attraction	

The particles of a liquid are always .... but there are forces of

.... between them. These forces prevent the particles moving

too far apart. The particles move at different .... If a particle

at the surface is moving .... enough it escapes the pull from the

particles below it. This is ....

Q3   Circle the correct words to complete these sentences.

a)   The attraction between particles in a liquid perfume is quite **weak** / **strong**.

b)   It is quite **difficult** / **easy** for the particles in a perfume to overcome attraction to other particles.

c)   How easily a liquid evaporates is known as its **volatility** / **solubility**.

Q4   Fabia is heating some soup. Explain why the smell of soup gets **stronger** as the liquid **warms up**.

....

....

....

Module C1 — Carbon Chemistry

Kinetic Theory and Forces Between Particles

Q5 Lucy tested chemicals X, Y and Z to see how suitable they were for use in liquid **air fresheners**.

A volunteer sat at one end of a room and a bottle containing the chemical was opened at the other end. She asked the volunteer to raise a hand when he or she **smelt** the chemical. The time between the bottle being opened and the volunteer's hand being raised was recorded. The test was repeated with different volunteers and the results are shown in the table below.

Chemical	Time (volunteer 1) /s	Time (volunteer 2) /s	Time (volunteer 3) /s	Average time /s
X	45	32	36	
Y	112	98	103	
Z	278	246	243	

a) Complete the table by working out the **average time** for each of the three chemicals.

b) Explain why the volunteers didn't smell the chemicals as soon as the bottles were opened.

....

....

....

c) What does the data tell you about the **volatility** of the chemicals? Circle your answer.

A — Liquid Y is the least volatile chemical.

B — Liquid X is the most volatile chemical.

C — Liquid Z is more volatile than liquid Y.

D — The tests don't tell you anything about volatility.

d) Suggest two more tests Lucy needs to carry out before any of the chemicals could be used in air fresheners.

....

....

Top Tip: Volatility is just a lovely word describing how easily a liquid evaporates. If a liquid is **volatile**, it evaporates **easily** — and it's likely to have a relatively low boiling point.

Solutions

Q1 Tick the correct boxes to show whether the following statements are **true** or **false**.

		True	False
a)	A solute is made by dissolving a solid in a liquid.	☐	☐
b)	A solvent is the liquid that the solid is dissolving into.	☐	☐
c)	A solution is a mixture of a solute and a solvent that doesn't separate out.	☐	☐
d)	A substance that will dissolve in a solvent is described as insoluble.	☐	☐
e)	Lots of esters make good solvents.	☐	☐

Q2 Read the following sentences and list all the **solutes**, **solvents** and **solutions** mentioned.

Salt dissolves in water to form brine. A tincture can be made by dissolving iodine in alcohol. Gold is soluble in mercury and this mixture is an amalgam.

a) Solutes ....

b) Solvents ....

c) Solutions ....

Q3 A chemical company is testing three new solvents for dry-cleaning.

a) What mass of solvent A is needed to dissolve 50 g of paint?

....

....

....

	Solvent		
	A	B	C
Cost per 100 g (£)	0.40	0.15	0.20
Solubility of paint (g per 100 g of solvent)	12.1	0.1	10.3

b) Which solvent would you choose to buy if you were a buyer for a dry-cleaning company? Explain your choice.

....

....

Q4 Circle the letters of any statements that correctly explain why **nail varnish** won't dissolve in **water**.

A Water is not a good solvent.

B The forces between the molecules of nail varnish are stronger than those between the molecules of water and the molecules of nail varnish.

C Water is only good for dissolving substances that are non-toxic.

D The forces between the molecules of water are stronger than those between the molecules of water and the molecules of nail varnish.

Module C1 — Carbon Chemistry

Paints and Pigments

Q1   Draw lines to match each term on the left with the correct description on the right.

pigment

colloid

solvent

binding medium

holds pigment particles to a surface

makes the paint thinner and easy to spread

tiny particles dispersed in another material

the substance that gives paint its colour

Q2   Which of the following statements are **true** and which are **false**?

		True	False
a)	A colloid is formed when solid particles dissolve into a liquid.	☐	☐
b)	Emulsion paints are colloids.	☐	☐
c)	Oil paints are colloids.	☐	☐
d)	The particles in colloids are always solids.	☐	☐
e)	The particles in colloids are so small that they stay dispersed and do not settle.	☐	☐

Q3   Circle the correct words to complete the sentences below.

a)   Gloss paints are **oil-based** / **water-based**. Emulsion paints are **oil-based** / **water-based**.

b)   Paint dries as the **solvent** / **binding medium** evaporates.

c)   In oil-based paints the solvent is **oil** / **something that dissolves oil**.

Q4   Ann is painting the outside of her front door using an **oil-based gloss paint**.
She brushes on a thin coat of paint and leaves it to dry for a whole day.

a)   Give one property of oil paint that would make it a good choice for painting a front door.

....

b)   Explain how an oil paint dries.

....

....

....

....

Special Pigments

Q1   **Thermochromic pigments** have many uses.

Suggest why themochromic pigments are suited to each of these uses:

a)   Colouring a spoon that is used for feeding a **baby**.

....

....

b)   Painting a design on a mug that is used for **hot drinks**.

....

....

Q2   Draw lines to join each statement to the **type of pigment** it relates to.

can become transparent
when heated

glow in the dark

**PHOSPHORESCENT
PIGMENTS**

used in thermometers

can be mixed with
acrylic paints to give a
wide range of colour changes

absorb and store energy and
release it as light

**THERMOCHROMIC
PIGMENTS**

used in
emergency exit signs

used in road signs

Q3   The diagram shows two watches with **glow-in-the-dark hands**.
One is from **1950**, the other is from **2006**.

1950   2006

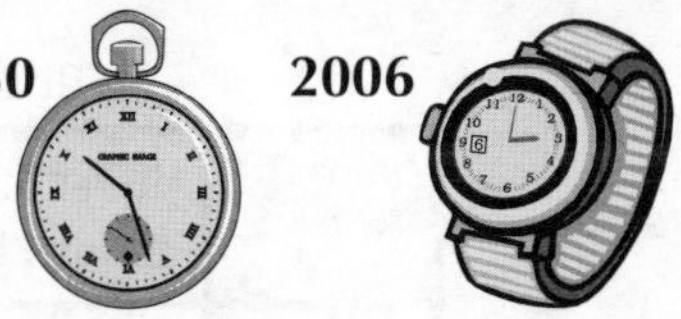

a)   Radioactive paint was used on the hands of the watch from 1950.
What type of paint was probably used on the watch from **2006**?

....

b)   Explain why the type of paint used was changed.

....

....

Polymers

Q1 Indicate whether the following sentences are **true** or **false**?

                                                                              True False

a) Making monomers from polymers is called polymerisation.

b) Alkene molecules are often used as the monomers.

c) Plastics are made up of lots of polymer chains.

d) The atoms within the polymer chains are held together by covalent bonds.

Q2 **Addition polymers** are formed when **unsaturated monomers** link together.

a) What is an unsaturated compound?

b) Name two conditions needed to make addition polymers.

Q3 The equation on the right shows the polymerisation of ethene to form **polyethene**.

$$n\left(\begin{array}{c}H\ \ H\\ |\ \ \ |\\ C=C\\ |\ \ \ |\\ H\ \ H\end{array}\right) \rightarrow \left(\begin{array}{c}H\ \ H\\ |\ \ \ |\\ C-C\\ |\ \ \ |\\ H\ \ H\end{array}\right)_n$$

many ethene molecules   polyethene

a) Draw a similar diagram in the box below to show the polymerisation of **propene** (C_3H_6).

It's easier if you think of propene as:

$$\begin{array}{c}H\ \ \ H\\ |\ \ \ \ |\\ C=C\\ |\ \ \ \ |\\ H\ \ CH_3\end{array}$$

b) Name the polymer you have drawn. ....

Q4 Nigel has two rulers made from **different plastics**. He first tries to bend them and then he heats them. The results are shown in the table.

	RESULT ON BENDING	RESULT ON HEATING
Ruler 1	Ruler bends easily and springs back into shape	Ruler becomes soft and then melts
Ruler 2	Ruler snaps in two	Ruler doesn't soften and eventually turns black

a) Which ruler is made from a polymer that has strong forces between its molecules? ....

b) Explain why the plastic used for Ruler 1 melts and bends easily.

Module C1 — Carbon Chemistry

Polymers and Their Uses

Q1 From the list below, underline any **properties** you think it is important for a plastic to have if it is to be used to make **Wellington boots**.

low melting point   waterproof   rigid   lightweight   heat-resistant

N.B. Chlorine dissolves spandex

Q2 Complete the table to show the most suitable **use** of each polymer using the options in the list.

carrier bags   kettles   window frames   disposable cups

POLYMER	PROPERTIES	USE
polypropene	heat-resistant	
polystyrene foam	thermal insulator	
low density polyethene	lightweight	
PVC	strong, durable, rigid	

Each use can only be used once.

Q3 Kate has three black jackets. One is made from **nylon**, another from nylon coated with **polyurethane**, and the third from a type of breathable fabric called **GORE-TEX®**.

a) Explain why the jacket coated with polyurethane would be better for Kate to wear on a rainy day than the plain nylon jacket.

....

b) Which jacket would you advise Kate to take for a week's hiking in Wales? Explain your answer.

....

....

c) The **GORE-TEX®** jacket is made from a thin film of another plastic called **expanded PTFE** laminated onto a layer of **nylon**. Explain how the two work together to give the material its useful properties.

....

....

....

Q4 Suggest a **problem** with each of the following methods of **disposing of plastics**.

a) Burial in landfill sites. ....

....

b) Burning. ....

....

c) Recycling. ....

....

Module C1 — Carbon Chemistry

Hydrocarbons — Alkanes

Q1   Look at the displayed formula of **Molecule X**, shown on the right.

$$\begin{array}{ccccc} & H & H & H & \\ & | & | & | & \\ H- & C- & C- & C- & H \\ & | & | & | & \\ & H & H & H & \end{array}$$

Molecule X

a)   Is molecule X a hydrocarbon? Explain your answer.

....

....

b)   Give the molecular formula of molecule X.

....

c)   The general formula for alkanes is C_nH_{2n+2}.
Is molecule X an alkane? Explain your answer.

....

....

d)   What is the name of molecule X? ....

Q2   Hydrocarbons such as **alkanes** are held together with **covalent** bonds.

a)   Tick the boxes to show if the following statements are **true** or **false**.

	True	False
i) Covalent bonds form when electrons are transferred from one atom to another.	☐	☐
ii) Covalent bonds form between atoms so that both have a full outer shell of electrons.	☐	☐
iii) Atoms can be joined by single or double covalent bonds.	☐	☐
iv) Alkanes are unsaturated compounds.	☐	☐
v) Alkanes won't form polymers.	☐	☐
vi) Ethane is an alkane molecule with a chain of four carbon atoms.	☐	☐

b)   How many covalent bonds do the following atoms make?

i) Carbon ....

ii) Hydrogen ....

Q3   The general formula for **alkanes** is C_nH_{2n+2}. Use this to write down the formulas of these alkanes.

a)   pentane (5 carbons) ....

b)   hexane (6 carbons)   ....

c)   octane (8 carbons)   ....

d)   dodecane (12 carbons) ....

Top Tip: These questions on hydrocarbons and alkanes shouldn't be too hard. Just make sure you don't confuse alkanes with alkenes — they're on the next page. Just what you wanted to hear...

Module C1 — Carbon Chemistry

Hydrocarbons — Alkenes

Q1 Complete this table showing the molecular and displayed formulas of some alkenes. If there's more than one possible displayed formula you only need to draw one correct example.

Alkene	Formula	Displayed formula
Ethene	**a)**	**b)**
c)	C_3H_6	**d)**
Butene	C_4H_8	**e)**

Q2 Tick the boxes to show if the statements are **true** or **false**?

		True	False
a)	Alkenes have double bonds between the hydrogen atoms.	☐	☐
b)	Alkenes are unsaturated.	☐	☐
c)	An unsaturated compound contains only single bonds.	☐	☐
d)	Alkenes are not very useful.	☐	☐
e)	Ethene has two carbon atoms.	☐	☐

Q3 Mark has two boiling tubes. One contains 20 cm³ of **hexane** and the other contains 20 cm³ of **hexene**. He also has a bottle of bromine water.

a) Describe how Mark can use the bromine water to tell the hexane and the hexene apart.

....

....

....

b) Name and describe the reaction that takes place between the hexene and the bromine water.

....

....

....

Fractional Distillation of Crude Oil

Q1   Circle the correct answer to each of the following questions.

a)   Why is crude oil called a fossil fuel?

   A — Because the oil is millions of years old.

      B — Because the oil was formed from animals and plants buried long ago.

      C — Because burning the fuel causes global warming.

b)   Why is crude oil non-renewable?

   A — It is impossible to create new oil.   B — Oil is very hard to find.

   C — Oil is being used up faster than it is being formed.

Q2   Circle the correct words to complete these sentences.

a)   Crude oil is a **mixture** / **compound** of different molecules.

b)   The molecules in crude oil are all **hydrocarbons** / **carbohydrates**.

c)   If crude oil were heated, the **first** / **last** fraction to be obtained would be bitumen.

d)   Diesel has **larger** / **smaller** molecules than petrol.

phwoar... nice tank, love

Q3   Label this diagram of a **fractionating column** to show where these substances can be collected.

   petrol   kerosene   diesel   oil   bitumen

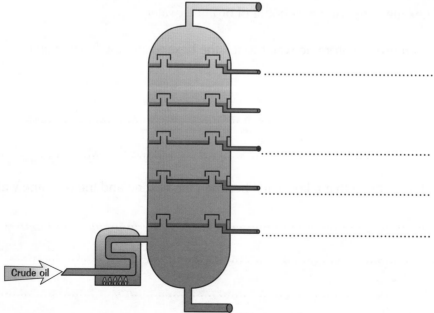

Crude oil

Fractional Distillation of Crude Oil

Q4   Crude oil is separated into different **fractions** by boiling.

a)   Put these crude oil fractions into order from highest to lowest boiling point.

> diesel   naphtha   kerosene   petrol

highest .... **lowest**

b)   Put the same fractions in order from most to least carbon atoms in their molecules.

most .... **least**

c)   Look at your answers for parts **a)** and **b)**. What is the connection between the number of carbon atoms in a molecule and its boiling point?

....

....

Q5   The following sentences describe how crude oil is separated by **fractional distillation**. Fill in the blanks in the sentences using some of the words below.

> high   gases   cooler   heated   smaller   low   bottom   hotter   fractions

A   Crude oil is .... causing most of the hydrocarbons to boil.

B   The hot .... rise up the fractionating column.

C   As they rise, the temperature begins to get ....

D   Near the .... of the column, large molecules with lots of carbon atoms condense first because they have .... boiling points.

E   As the gases rise further and become cooler, ... molecules with lower boiling points turn into liquids.

F   In this way crude oil is separated into ...., which are mixtures of only a few different hydrocarbons, with similar numbers of carbon atoms and similar boiling points.

Top Tip: Fractional distillation can be a tricky idea to get your head round, but once you do you'll be able to answer anything they throw at you. Learn the order of the fractions too, they love that.

Module C1 — Carbon Chemistry

Hydrocarbon Properties — Bonds

Q1 During **fractional distillation** hydrocarbons are separated using their **boiling points**.

a) Explain the trend in the boiling points of alkanes in terms of **intermolecular forces**.

....

....

....

b) Explain why the hydrocarbon molecules do not breakdown into hydrogen and carbon atoms when they are heated during fractional distillation.

....

....

Q2 Here is a table showing the properties of some **alkanes**.

Alkane	Melting point (°C)	Boiling point (°C)
Methane (CH_4)	−182	−162
Pentane (C_5H_{12})	−130	36
Hexane (C_6H_{14})	−95	69
Decane ($C_{10}H_{22}$)	−30	174
Octadecane ($C_{18}H_{38}$)	28	317

a) Which of these alkanes are liquids at room temperature (25 °C)?

....

b) Which of these liquids is the most volatile? ....

c) Which alkane will be a solid at room temperature? ....

d) Which of the liquids will flow most easily along a pipe? ....

Q3 Jim investigated how the **size** of a hydrocarbon molecule affects its **volatility**. He took 50 cm³ of each of three different hydrocarbons and put them into evaporating basins. He left them for five hours and then measured how much of each was left. His results are shown in the table below.

No. of C atoms	Initial vol. (cm³)	Vol. after 5 hours (cm³)	Vol. lost (cm³)
6	50	8	
10	50	37	
12	50	48	

a) Complete the table by filling in the volume of each hydrocarbon that has evaporated.

b) If this is to be a fair test, what must be kept the same for all three hydrocarbons (apart from using the same volume of each)?

Think what could affect how fast the liquids evaporate.

....

c) What can Jim conclude about volatility and the size of hydrocarbons?

....

....

Cracking

Q1 Fill in the gaps using the words below.

| high | shorter | longer | catalyst | cracking | diesel | low | molecules | petrol |

There is more need for .... chain fractions of crude oil such

as .... than for .... chain fractions such as

.... Heating long hydrocarbon molecules to ....

temperatures with a .... breaks them down into smaller

.... This is called ....

Q2 Circle the correct answer for each of the following questions.

a) What type of chemical reaction is cracking?

A — Neutralisation   **B** — Displacement

C — Thermal decomposition   **D** — Redox

b) Why are high temperatures needed to crack alkanes?

A — Catalysts only work when hot.   **B** — Energy is needed to break strong covalent bonds.

C — Large alkane molecules have strong intermolecular forces.

D — Alkenes are very unreactive hydrocarbons.

Q3 Cracking produces different types of **useful molecules**.

a) Name the two types of molecule you get from cracking a long-chain hydrocarbon.

....

b) A molecule produced in the cracking process has the formula C_2H_4.

i) What is the name of this hydrocarbon? ....

ii) What is the main use of C_2H_4? ....

c) Name two conditions needed to crack liquid paraffin in the lab.

....

Top Tips: Cracking is really useful, and dead important too. It helps us get the most out of crude oil, so we don't end up with loads of a fraction that we don't want or need. Hooray for cracking!

Module C1 — Carbon Chemistry

Cracking

Q4   Change this diagram into a **word equation** and a **symbol equation**.

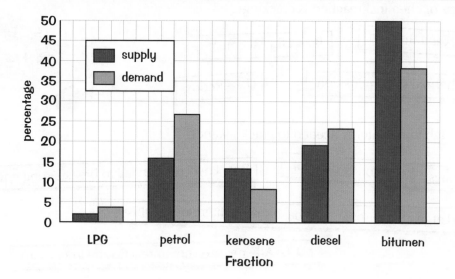

a)   Word equation: .... → .... + ...

b)   Symbol equation: .... → .... + ...

Q5   Horatio owns a **crude oil refinery**. He records the amount of each fraction that's **present** in a sample of crude oil and compares it against how much of each fraction his customers want.

a)   Which fractions in this sample of crude oil are in excess (more is produced than can be sold)?

....

b)   For which fraction in this sample does the demand outweigh the supply by the greatest amount?

....

c)   Explain how cracking will help Horatio match the levels of supply to the levels of demand.

....

....

d)   Suggest how else cracking can benefit crude oil companies economically.

....

....

Module C1 — Carbon Chemistry

Use of Fossil Fuels

Q1   Circle the correct words to complete the passage below.

We rely on crude oil to provide us with **energy / metals** and as a source of raw materials for making chemicals. Because crude oil is a **renewable / non-renewable** resource it will eventually run out. As it becomes scarcer the price of oil will **increase / decrease** and everything that relies on oil as a raw material or fuel for its production will become **more expensive / cheaper**.

Q2   The amount of fossil fuels being burnt worldwide is **increasing** every year.

a)   Give one reason why the amount of fossil fuels being burnt is increasing.

....

b)   Some countries only have very small reserves of fossil fuels.
Describe the political problems associated with having to import oil.

....

....

....

Q3   Complete the passage using some of the words given below.

| detergents | field | waterproof | cold | slick | absorbent | heat | toxic | coagulants |

If a tanker carrying crude oil is damaged the oil spills into the sea creating an oil ....

If any of this oil gets onto the feathers of seabirds it stops them from being ....

Birds that are contaminated in this way often die of ....

Sometimes .... are added to spilled oil in an attempt to disperse it, but these can

be .... to marine wildlife, like fish and shellfish.

Q4   Isobella is trying to decide which hydrocarbon, A or B, is the best one to use as a fuel.
She tests the **energy content** of the hydrocarbons by using them to heat 50 cm³ of water from 25 °C to 40 °C. The results of this experiment are shown in the table.

Hydrocarbon	Initial Mass (g)	Final Mass (g)	Mass of Fuel Burnt (g)
A	98	92	
B	102	89	

a)   Complete the table by calculating the mass of fuel that was burned in each case.

b)   Which fuel contains more energy per gram? ....

c)   Name two other things Isobella should consider when choosing the best fuel to use.

....

Burning Fuels

Q1   Hydrocarbons make good **fuels**.

a)   Write a **general word equation** for completely burning a hydrocarbon in the open air.

....

b)   Write **balanced symbol equations** for completely burning these alkanes in open air:

i) methane, CH_4 ....

ii) propane, C_3H_8 ....

Q2   Describe how the apparatus on the right could be used to show that water and carbon dioxide are produced when **hexane** (a hydrocarbon) is completely burned.

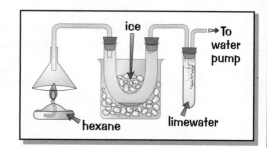

....

....

....

....

Q3   **Incomplete combustion** can cause problems.

a)   Does **complete** or **incomplete** combustion release more energy?

....

b)   Complete the balanced symbol equations for the incomplete combustion of butane:

i) to produce carbon monoxide.

$$2\ C_4H_{10}\ +\ ....\ \rightarrow\ ....\ H_2O\ +\ ....\ CO$$

ii) to produce carbon.

$$2\ C_4H_{10}\ +\ ....\ \rightarrow\ ....\ H_2O\ +\ ....\ C$$

c)   Why is incomplete combustion:

i) dangerous? ....

ii) a waste of fuel? ....

iii) messy? ....

Module C1 — Carbon Chemistry

The Evolution of the Atmosphere

Q1   Tick the boxes next to the sentences below that are **true**.

When the Earth was formed, its surface was molten. ☐

The Earth's early atmosphere is thought to have been mostly oxygen. ☐

When oxygen started building up in the atmosphere, all organisms began to thrive. ☐

The early atmosphere was mostly made up of gases that had escaped from inside the Earth during volcanic eruptions. ☐

Q2   The amount of **carbon dioxide** in the atmosphere has changed over the last 4.5 billion or so years.

Describe how the level of carbon dioxide has changed and explain why this change happened.

....

....

....

....

Q3   Draw lines to put the statements in the **right order** on the timeline.   One has been done for you.

Present

NOT TO SCALE

4500 million years ago

The Earth cooled down slightly. A thin crust formed.

Water vapour condensed to form oceans.

The Earth formed. There was lots of volcanic activity.

More complex organisms evolved.

Plant life appeared.

The atmosphere is about four-fifths nitrogen and one-fifth oxygen.

Oxygen builds up in the air as plants photosynthesise.

Don't get confused — 4500 million is the same as 4.5 billion.

The Evolution of the Atmosphere

Q4   The pie chart below shows the proportions of different gases in the Earth's atmosphere today.

a)   Add the labels '**Nitrogen**', '**Oxygen**', and '**Carbon dioxide and other gases**'.

Earth's Atmosphere Today

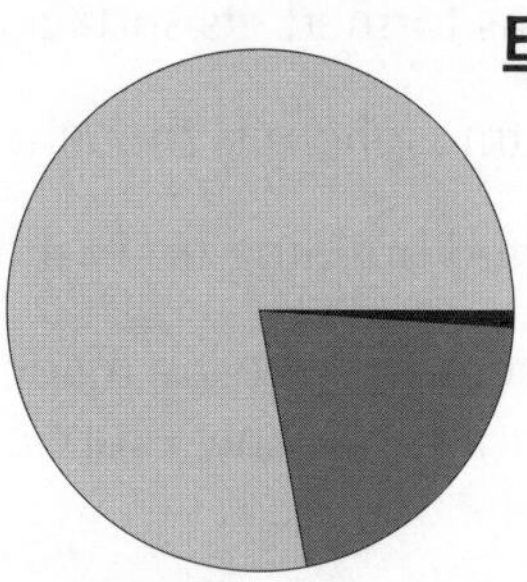

b)   Give the approximate percentages of the following gases in the air today:

Nitrogen ....

Oxygen ....

Carbon dioxide ....

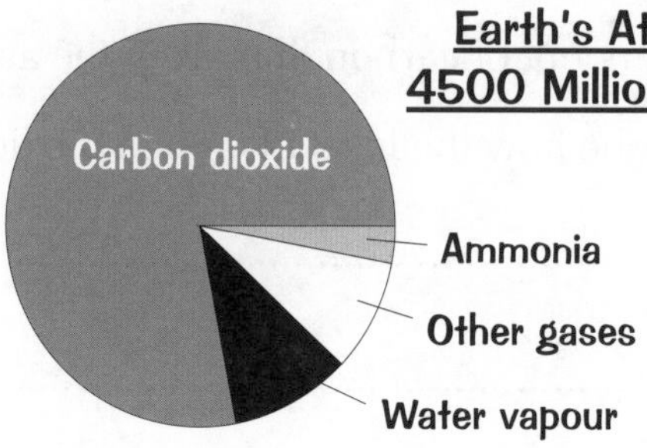

c)   This pie chart shows the proportions of different gases that we think were in the Earth's atmosphere 4500 million years ago.

Earth's Atmosphere 4500 Million Years Ago

Carbon dioxide

Ammonia

Other gases

Water vapour

Describe the main differences between today's atmosphere and the atmosphere 4500 million years ago.

....

....

d)   Explain why the amount of water vapour has decreased.

....

What did the water vapour change into?

....

e)   Explain how oxygen was introduced into the atmosphere.

....

f)   Give two effects of the oxygen levels in the atmosphere rising.

1. ....

....

2. ....

....

g)   Explain why the percentage of nitrogen gas in the air has increased so much.

....

....

....

Module C1 — Carbon Chemistry

The Carbon Cycle

Q1 Here is a diagram of the **carbon cycle**.

a) What is process A? ....

b) What is process B? ....

c) Process C could be decay. What else could it be?

....

d) What is substance D? ....

Q2 The **human population** is increasing rapidly and this increase is affecting the atmosphere.

List two reasons why this dramatic increase in population has caused a rise in CO_2 levels.

....

....

Sid's day

8.00 am: Wakes up, fills his kettle to the top and makes a cup of tea to enjoy with a pineapple, which was grown in Ghana.
10.00 am: Drives to the travel agent in his shiny new 4X4 car and books a holiday in Hawaii departing that evening.
11.00 am: Goes shopping for a grass skirt.
11.30 am: Returns home and decides to put on his grass skirt. But it's a bit chilly, so he puts the heating on high.
5.00 pm: Leaves for the airport, leaving all the lights on to keep burglars away.

Q3 On the left is some information about what Sid does one day.

Suggest three ways that Sid could have lowered the amount of carbon dioxide he produced.

....

....

....

....

Q4 **Deforestation** increases the amount of **carbon dioxide** released into the atmosphere and decreases the amount removed.

a) Give two reasons why deforestation causes carbon dioxide to be added to the atmosphere.

....

....

b) Why does deforestation reduce the amount of CO_2 removed from the atmosphere?

....

Top Tips: It's tough minimising your carbon emissions when you live in a world of cheap flights, abundant plastic bags, supermarkets filled with cheap exotic food, and central heating. But if we carry on the way we're going, the world's likely to be in a lot of trouble one day.

Module C1 — Carbon Chemistry

Air Pollution and Acid Rain

Q1 Use the words and phrases below to complete the paragraph.

nitric   global warming   sulfuric   nitrogen oxides   acid rain

When fossil fuels are burned carbon dioxide is produced. The main problem caused

by this is .... The gas sulfur dioxide is also produced.

When it combines with moisture in the air .... acid is produced.

This falls as acid rain. In the high temperatures inside a car engine nitrogen and oxygen

from the air react together to produce .... These react with moisture

to make .... acid, which is another cause of acid rain.

Q2 **Pollutants** from burning fossil fuels cause a variety of problems.

a) Why might architects choose **not** to build from limestone in polluted cities?

....

b) Give **two** other consequences of acid rain.

....

c) Briefly describe how photochemical smog is formed.

....

....

Q3 **Catalytic converters** reduce the amount of harmful gases that are released into the atmosphere.

a) Complete the following equations to show a reaction that occurs in a catalytic converter:

i) carbon monoxide + nitrogen oxide → .... + ...

ii) ....CO + ...NO → .... + ...

b) What catalyst is usually used for this reaction? ....

c) Why is carbon monoxide so dangerous?

....

....

Module C1 — Carbon Chemistry

Mixed Questions — Module C1

Q1 **Baking powder** is often one of the ingredients in cakes.

a) Baking powder contains sodium hydrogen carbonate.

i) Sodium hydrogen carbonate can be produced by reacting soda ash with water and carbon dioxide. Balance the equation below that shows this process.

.... Na_2CO_3 + ... CO_2 + ... H_2O $\rightarrow$ .... $NaHCO_3$

ii) Explain why sodium hydrogen carbonate is a useful addition to a cake mix.

....

....

b) The cake mix fills the bottom of the tin that it is poured into, but when cooked, the cake no longer flows. Explain why this is in terms of the **movement** of the particles and the **forces** between them.

....

....

Q2 **Chloroethene** (C_2H_3Cl) is used to make the addition polymer, **polychloroethene** (**PVC**).

a) Chloroethene is produced from ethene. Ethene is commonly made by thermal decomposition of long-chain hydrocarbons. What is the name for this process?

....

b) What feature does chloroethene have that allows it to form an addition polymer?

....

c) Write an equation in the space on the right for the polymerisation of chloroethene, using **displayed formulae** to show the structure of chloroethene and the repeating unit in PVC.

d) PVC can be used to make plastic pipes and guttering. Suggest **two** properties that a plastic should have if it is going to be used to make guttering.

....

e) PVC is **non-biodegradable**.

i) Explain what this means.

....

ii) Suggest why chemists are working to produce polymers that do biodegrade.

....

Mixed Questions — Module C1

Q3   Nail varnish does **not** dissolve in water. This is important, otherwise every time a person washed their hands it would wash away.

a)   Explain, in terms of the molecules, why nail varnish does not dissolve in water.

....

b)   Explain, in terms of the molecules, how nail varnish remover removes the varnish.

....

c)   The active chemical in nail varnish is a **volatile liquid**.

i)   Explain what "**volatile**" means.

....

ii)   Explain, in terms of the particles, what happens when this chemical **evaporates** from the nails.

....

....

iii) Name **another product** that must be **volatile** in order to work effectively. Explain why this is.

....

....

Q4   **Fuel X** is a hydrocarbon that can be burnt to release energy.
A company is trying to decide whether or not to use fuel X to power its machinery.

a)   Give two properties of fuel X, other than its energy value, that the company should take into account when deciding whether or not to use it industrially.

1. ....

2. ....

b)   Fuel X contains only hydrogen and carbon.
What could the products of the reaction include when fuel X is burnt:

i) in plentiful oxygen ....

ii) in low oxygen ....

c)   A research scientist at the company burns a small quantity of the fuel to determine its energy value. If he burns it in a plentiful supply of oxygen, what colour will the flame be?

....

Mixed Questions — Module C1

Q5 Crude oil is a mixture of hydrocarbons, which is separated by **fractional distillation** into useful fractions.

a) i) Label the **diesel** and **naphtha** fractions on the diagram.

ii) Which fraction has the higher boiling point?
Underline the correct answer.

naphtha   **diesel**

iii) Why does this fraction have a higher boiling point?

....

....

....

[Diagram of fractional distillation column with outputs labelled: Refinery gas (bottled gas), Petrol, ..., Kerosene, ..., Oil, Bitumen. Input labelled: Crude oil]

b) Explain how the fractions are separated in fractional distillation.

....

....

c) Explain why plastic products may become much more expensive in the future.

....

....

Q6 The atmosphere of Mars consists of 95.3% carbon dioxide, 2.7% nitrogen, and 2% of other gases.

a) Describe the similarities between this and the early atmosphere of Earth.

....

....

b) Describe the differences between the compositions of the atmospheres of Mars and Earth today.

....

....

c) Describe how human activity is affecting the composition of the air.

....

....

....

Moving and Storing Heat

Q1   Complete these sentences by circling the correct word from each pair.

Heat is a measure of **hotness** / **energy**.

Temperature is a measure of **hotness** / **energy**.

Heat travels from a **hot** / **cold** place to a **hot** / **cold** place.

Water is a good material for storing heat because it has a **high** / **low** specific heat capacity.

When a substance is heated its particles vibrate **more** / **less** quickly.

Q2   **Temperature** can be measured on various **scales**.

a) Give an example of a scale used to measure temperature. ....

b) Everyday **temperature** scales go **lower than zero**. Explain why
it isn't possible to have a measurement of **heat** that is below zero.

....

....

Q3 **a)** What is **specific heat capacity**?

....

b) Agatha has 1 kg samples of two substances — A and B. Substance **A** has a
higher specific heat capacity than substance B. Both samples cool down
by 10 °C. Which will release more heat — A or B? Circle the correct answer.

Substance A

Substance B

Q4   Mildred thinks she could make her hot water bottle more efficient by filling it with **mercury**, which
has a specific heat capacity of **139 J/kg /°C** . The specific heat capacity of water is **4200 J/kg /°C**.

Work out the **difference** in energy released by two litres of mercury cooling
from 70 °C to 20 °C and two litres of water cooling from 70 °C to 20 °C .
(2 l of mercury has a mass of 27.2 kg. 2 l of water has a mass of 2 kg.)

*Don't try this at home
— mercury's toxic at
any temperature.*

....

....

....

Q5   A piece of copper is heated to **90 °C** and then lowered into a beaker of water which is at **20 °C**.
The copper transfers **3040 J** of energy to the water before it is removed. The temperature of the
copper after it is removed is **50 °C**. The specific heat capacity of copper is **380 J/kg/°C**.

Calculate the **mass** of the copper. ....

....

Melting and Boiling

Q1 The graph shows the temperature change as a substance is heated up.
The letters A to E represent each **state** of the substance and each **change of state**.

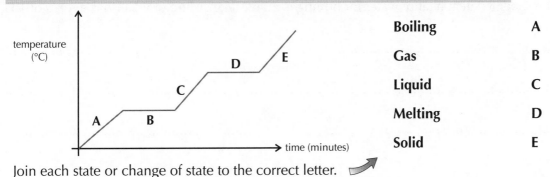

Boiling	A
Gas	B
Liquid	C
Melting	D
Solid	E

Join each state or change of state to the correct letter.

Q2 A beaker of pure water is heated. When it reaches 100 °C it **stays** at 100 °C, even though it is **still being heated**. Which of sentences A-D is the correct explanation for why this happens? Circle the correct letter.

A   Energy is being lost to the surroundings as quickly as it is being supplied to the beaker.

B   The pan is absorbing the extra energy.

C   The energy supplied is being used to break intermolecular bonds and change the water to steam.

D   A more powerful heater should have been used.

Q3 The graph shows what happens to the temperature of a beaker of **molten wax** as it cools to room temperature.

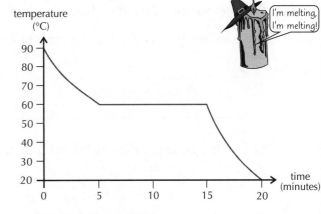

a) At what temperature does the wax become **solid** again?

....

b) Explain why the temperature of the wax **remains constant** during solidification.

....

....

c) From the start of solidification, **how long** did it take before all the liquid wax became solid?

....

Top Tips:
The next page has some nice **sums** all about melting and boiling. Melting and boiling calculations always involve **specific latent heat** — definitely not to be confused with **specific heat capacity**. Remember, while a substance is changing state, its temperature doesn't change. So don't try to use a formula with 'temperature change' in it for melting or boiling sums — it won't work.

Melting and Boiling

Q4 A kettle supplies energy at a rate of **2500 J per second**. It contains 1.5 litres of water which is at 100 °C. **How long** would the kettle need to boil for in order to **evaporate** all this water? (The specific latent heat of water for boiling is 2.26 MJ/kg. 1 litre of water has a mass of 1 kg.)

....

....

....

Q5 Answer the following questions using the information in the table.

Substance	Melting Point (°C)	Specific latent heat of melting (kJ/kg)
Water (ice)	0	334
Aluminium	658	396
Copper	1083	205
Lead	327	23
Zinc	419	110

a) A heater supplies **500 kJ** of thermal energy over **10 minutes**.

  i) Use the table to calculate the **mass of ice** at 0 °C that it could melt in 10 minutes.

  ....

  ....

  ii) Use the table to calculate the **mass of zinc** at 419 °C that it could melt in 10 minutes.

  ....

  ....

b) Dave puts **ice** in his lemonade to cool it down. The ice melts.
Calculate the energy transferred to **30 g** of ice cubes by **300 g** of lemonade as the ice melts.

  ....

c) A heater supplies energy to **2 kg of lead** at 20 °C. The energy supplied is used to increase its temperature. The temperature of the lead keeps increasing and then stays at the **same temperature**. While the lead stays at the same temperature, what is the energy supplied **used** for?

  ....

Conduction and Convection in the Home

Q1 Tick to show whether the sentences are true or false.

True False

a) Conduction involves **energy** passing between **vibrating particles**. ☐ ☐

b) Some **metals** are very **poor** conductors. ☐ ☐

c) **Solids** are usually better **conductors** of heat than liquids and gases. ☐ ☐

d) **Plastic** is a **poor** conductor because it contains **free electrons**. ☐ ☐

Q2 George picks up a piece of wood and a metal spoon. Both are at the same temperature: 20 °C.

Explain why the metal spoon feels **colder** to the touch than the piece of wood.

....

....

Q3 Match each observation with an explanation.

The very bottom of a hot water tank stays cold...

because water isn't a good heat conductor.

Warm air rises...

because heat flows from warm places to cooler ones.

A small heater can send heat all over a room...

because it is not so dense.

Q4 Sam uses the apparatus shown to investigate **heat transfer** in water.

He heats the middle of the tube with a Bunsen flame. The ice at the top of the tube melts quickly, but the ice at the bottom does not melt.

Ice floating at the top

Glass tube full of cold water

Ice weighted so it stays at the bottom

What does this experiment show about conduction and convection in water? Explain your answer.

....

....

....

Q5 Great Aunt Marjorie knits blankets for babies. She says that a blanket **with holes** in keeps a baby **warmer** than a blanket without holes in. Why is this?

....

....

Heat Radiation

Q1 Tick the sentences below to show whether they are **true** or **false**.

		True	False
a)	The amount of heat radiation absorbed by a surface depends only on its colour.	☐	☐
b)	The hotter a surface is, the more heat it radiates.	☐	☐
c)	Heat is radiated as ultraviolet waves.	☐	☐
d)	All objects are constantly absorbing and emitting heat radiation.	☐	☐
e)	Heat radiation can travel through a vacuum.	☐	☐

Q2 Mr Jones and Ms Smith each put a **solar hot water panel** on the roof of their houses.

Explain why Ms Smith gets more hot water than Mr Jones.

Ms Smith's house

Mr Jones' house

....

....

Q3 Complete the following by circling the correct word from each pair.

a) **Dark**, **matt** surfaces are **good / poor** absorbers and **good / poor** emitters of heat radiation.

b) The best surfaces for **radiating** heat are **good / poor** absorbers and **good / poor** emitters.

c) The best surfaces for **solar hot water panels** are **good / poor** absorbers and **good / poor** emitters.

Q4 Paul is making beans on toast with sausages for tea. He notices that the outside of the bread **darkens** as it toasts.

You're far too young to be smoking.

a) How is **energy transferred** from the element in the toaster to the bread? ....

b) The **middle** of the bread will also warm up, but much more **slowly** than the outside. Explain why.

....

....

c) Paul lines his grill pan with **shiny foil**. How does this help him **grill sausages** more effectively?

....

....

d) He heats some beans in the microwave oven. Briefly explain how microwaves heat up the beans.

....

....

Saving Energy

Q1 Heat is lost from a house through its **roof**, **walls**, **doors** and **windows**.

a) In the spaces on the diagram, write down one measure that could be taken to reduce heat losses through each part of the house. An example has been done for you.

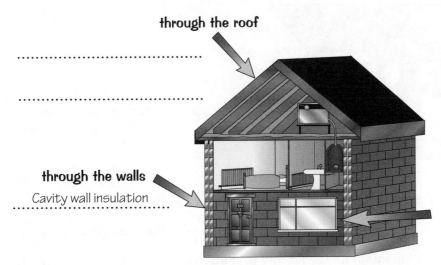

through the roof

....

....

through the windows

....

....

through the walls

Cavity wall insulation

....

b) Explain how heat can still be lost though the walls of a house with cavity wall insulation.

....

....

....

Q2 Mr Tarantino wants to buy a **hot water tank jacket** to save on his heating bills, but his friend tells him that **loft insulation** would be more **cost-effective**.

	Hot water tank jacket	Loft insulation
Initial Cost	£60	£200
Annual Saving	£15	£100
Payback time	4 years	

a) Calculate the **payback time** for loft insulation and write it in the table.

b) Is the friend's advice correct? Give reasons for your answer.

....

....

Top Tips: Saving energy in the home is mostly to do with reducing heat loss — so making sure you don't have to use more energy to make more heat to replace the stuff you've lost. It doesn't have to be expensive — even a thicker pair of curtains at the window will help a bit.

<u>*Saving Energy*</u>

Q3 A **thermogram** can show where heat energy is escaping from a house.

Study the thermogram of three terraced houses **X**, **Y** and **Z** below.
For each description below, write the correct letter **X**, **Y** or **Z** in the box.

X   Y   Z

*For each description, think about where
the most heat would be lost and match
this up to the key on the picture.*

least heat lost ——————————➤   most heat lost

a) This house has good loft and window insulation but poor wall insulation.

b) This house has double glazing and cavity wall insulation, but poor loft insulation.

c) This house has good thick loft insulation and cavity wall insulation
but it has poorly insulated windows with no double glazing.

Q4 Draw arrows to match up the **words** with their **meanings**.

Cost

Cost-effectiveness

Payback time

Effectiveness

How much energy you save.

How much you have to pay.

How long it takes to save as much as you spent initially.

How worthwhile it is to spend the money.

Q5 Explain how the following types of insulation work.

a) Cavity wall insulation ....

....

b) Loft insulation ....

....

c) Double glazing ....

....

Efficiency

Q1 Tick the boxes to show whether these statements are **true** or **false**.

	True	False

a) The **total energy supplied** to a machine is called the **input**. ☐ ☐

b) The **useful output** of a machine is never more than its total input. ☐ ☐

c) The **energy output** of a machine is the **useful energy** it delivers. ☐ ☐

d) The more **efficient** a machine is, the more energy it **wastes**. ☐ ☐

Q2 Complete the following **energy transfer diagrams** to show the **useful** energy output of various devices. The first one has been done for you.

A solar water heating panel: light energy → heat energy

a) A gas cooker: .... → heat energy

b) A television screen : electrical energy → ....

c) An electric buzzer: .... → ....

Efficiency = Useful Energy Output ÷ Energy Input

Q3 Use the **efficiency formula** to complete the table.

Total Energy Input (J)	Useful Energy Output (J)	Efficiency
2000	1500	
	2000	0.50
4000		0.25
600	200	

Q4 Tina was investigating a model **winch** — a machine that uses an electric motor to lift objects.

Tina calculated that, in theory, **10 J** of electrical energy would be needed to lift a **boot** 50 cm off a table. She then tried lifting the boot with the winch and found that **20 J** of electrical energy was used.

Why did the winch use so much electrical energy in practice? In your answer, include an explanation of what happened to the 'extra' 10 joules.

....

....

....

Sankey Diagrams

Q1 Professor Bean is testing a new **high-efficiency** car engine.
He finds that for every 100 J of energy supplied to the engine, 75 J are transformed into **kinetic energy** in the moving car, 5 J are wasted as **sound energy** and the rest is turned into **heat energy**.

On the graph paper below, draw a **Sankey diagram** to illustrate his results.

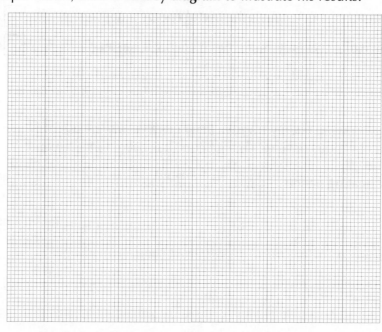

Q2 The Sankey diagram below is for a **winch** — a machine which **lifts** objects on hooks and cables.

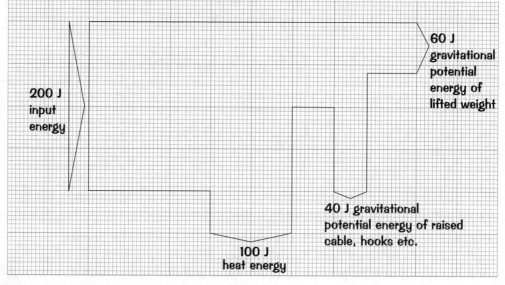

200 J input energy

60 J gravitational potential energy of lifted weight

40 J gravitational potential energy of raised cable, hooks etc.

100 J heat energy

a) What is the total amount of energy **wasted**? .... J

b) How much useful **gravitational energy** is produced? .... J

c) Calculate the **efficiency** of the winch. Give your answer as a decimal.

Efficiency = Useful Energy Output ÷ Energy Input

....

....

Wave Basics

Q1 Diagrams A, B and C represent **electromagnetic waves**.

A   **B**   **C**

a) Which two diagrams show waves with the same **frequency**? ...... and ......

b) Which two diagrams show waves with the same **amplitude**? ...... and ......

c) Which two diagrams show waves with the same **wavelength**? ...... and ......

Q2 A ripple in a pond travels at **0.5 m/s**. It makes a duck bob up and down **twice every second**.

a) What is the **frequency** of the duck's bobbing? ....

Remember what's meant by a wavelength, then use $v = f\lambda$.

b) When the duck is on the crest of a wave, **how far away** is the next crest?

....

Q3 **Green light** travels at 3×10^8 m/s and has a wavelength of about 5×10^{-7} m.

Calculate the **frequency** of green light. Give the correct unit in your answer.

You'll have to use $v = f\lambda$.

....

....

Q4 Radio waves travel at the **speed of light** (300 000 000 m/s).
Radio 3 has a **frequency** of **90 MHz**.

a) Write down the speed of light in **standard form**. ....

b) Write the **frequency** in Hz in standard form. ....

c) Calculate the **wavelength** of these radio waves. Give your answer in m.

Be careful with units.

....

Q5 Put the following frequencies in order of **size**, from the **highest** frequency to the **lowest** frequency.

90 MHz   900 kHz   9 000 000 Hz 9×10^4 Hz 9×10^2 MHz

It'll help if you put them all into hertz, and in standard form.

....

Wave Properties

Q1   Harriet spends at least an hour looking at herself in a **mirror** every day.
The image she sees is formed from light reflected by the mirror.

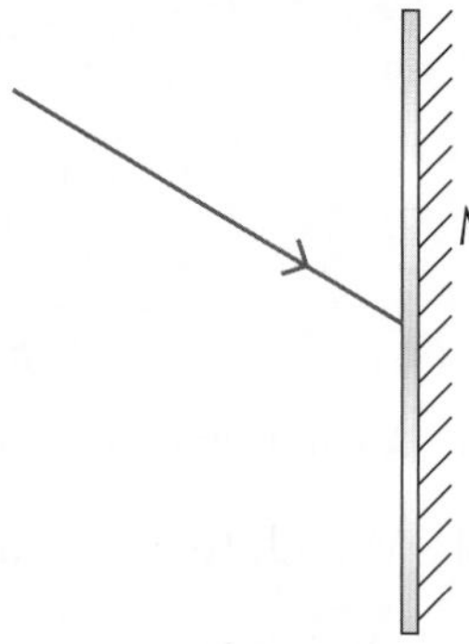

a)   What is meant by a "normal" when talking about reflection?

....

....

b)   Complete the diagram to show an incident ray of light being
reflected by the mirror. Label the **angle of incidence**, **i**,
the **normal**, and the **angle of reflection**, **r**.

Mirror

Q2   Tick the boxes to show whether these statements are **true** or **false**.

		True	False
a)	EM waves travel in **straight lines** through **different substances**.	☐	☐
b)	The **normal** is at right angles to the **incident ray**.	☐	☐
c)	The **angle of incidence** is always equal to the **angle of reflection**.	☐	☐
d)	Total internal reflection only happens when a ray passes from a **less dense** substance, to a **more dense** substance.	☐	☐

Q3   The diagrams show rays of light in an **optical fibre**.
Draw arrows to match each diagram to the correct description of what is happening.

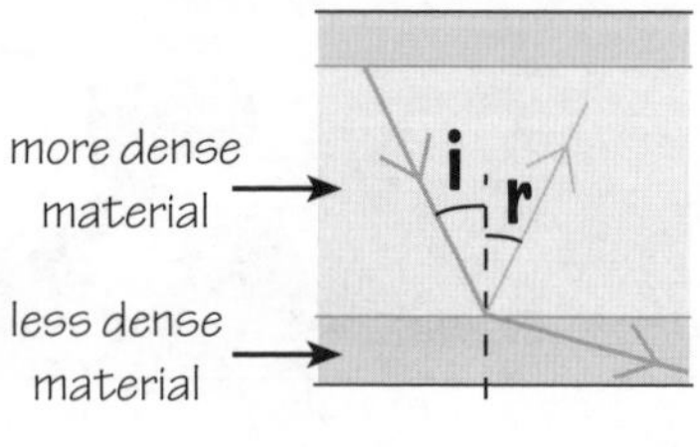

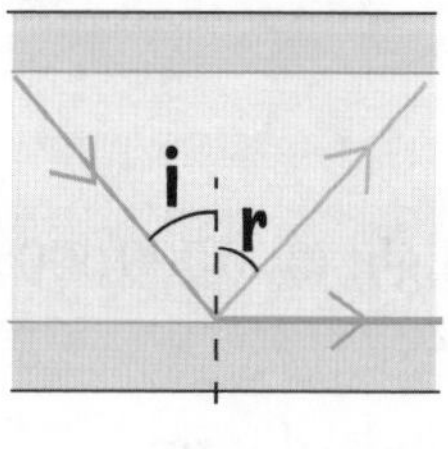

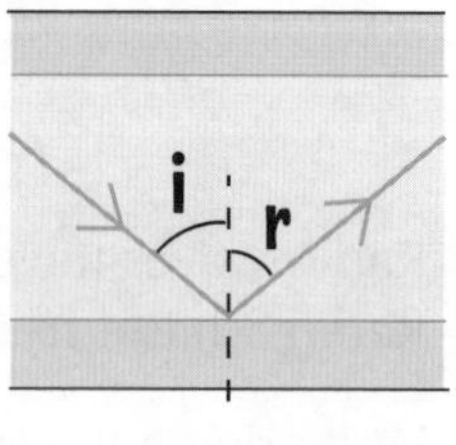

more dense
material

less dense
material

Total internal reflection

**Most of the light passes
out of the optical fibre, but
some is reflected internally.**

**Most of the light is reflected
internally, but some emerges
along the surface of the glass.**

Q4   Explain what is meant by the **'critical angle'** for a boundary between two materials.

....

....

Module P1 — Energy for the Home

Diffraction and Refraction

Q1   An important property of waves is **diffraction**.

a) Explain what 'diffraction' means.

....

....

b) A ripple tank is used to study the behaviour of waves as they pass through gaps. The gap in diagram 1 is about the **same size** as the wavelength. The gap in diagram 2 is **much bigger**. Complete both diagrams to show what happens to the waves after they pass through the gaps.

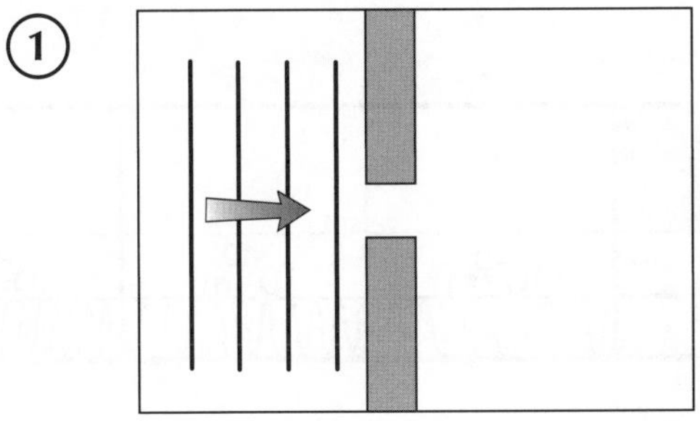

①

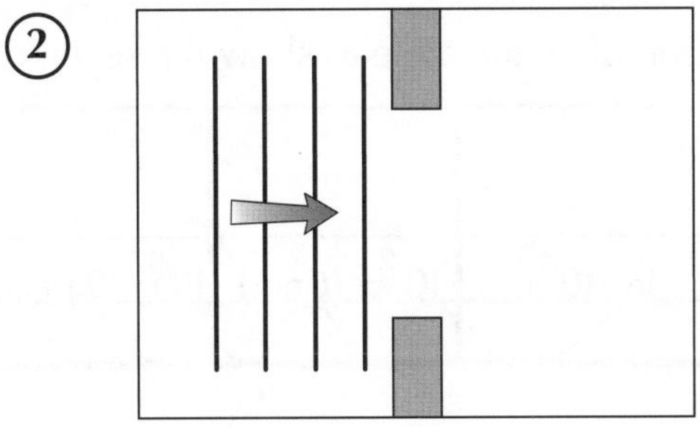

②

Q2   Diagrams A and B show waves travelling from a **less dense** medium to a **denser** medium.

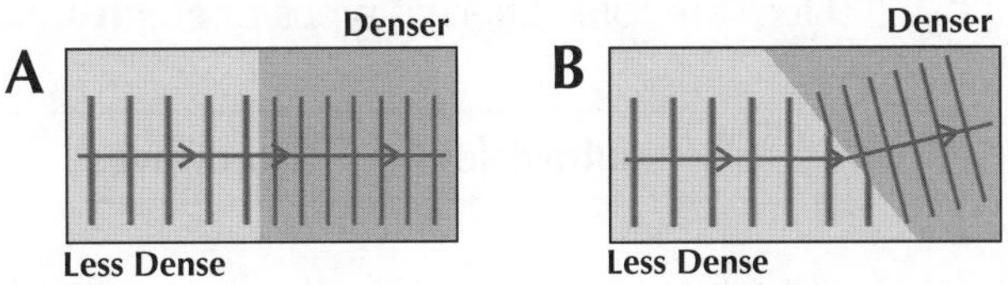

a) Which diagram shows the waves being **refracted**? ....

b) Why does refraction **not happen** in the other diagram?

....

c) What happens to the **wavelength** of the waves as they pass into the denser medium?

....

d) What happens to the **frequency** of the waves as they pass into the denser medium?

....

e) What happens to the **velocity** of the waves as they pass into the denser medium?

....

f) Imagine that the wave in the denser medium in diagram B passes into a **less dense** medium again. What would you expect to happen to the wave?   *Think about wavelength, frequency and speed.*

....

....

EM Waves and Communication

Q1 Indicate whether the following statements are true or false.

True False

a) Visible light travels faster in a vacuum than both X-rays and radio waves. ☐ ☐

b) All EM waves transfer matter from place to place. ☐ ☐

c) Radio waves have the shortest wavelength of all EM waves. ☐ ☐

d) All EM waves can travel through space. ☐ ☐

Q2 EM radiation occurs at many different wavelengths.

Complete the table to show the seven types of EM waves:

			VISIBLE LIGHT			
1m-10^4m	10^{-2}m (3cm)	10^{-5}m (0.01mm)	10^{-7}m	10^{-8}m	10^{-10}m	10^{-12}m

Q3 Here are four different types of **electromagnetic wave**:

ultraviolet	microwaves	X-rays	infrared

a) Which has the **lowest frequency**? ....

b) Which carries the **most energy**? ....

c) Which **two** are used for **wireless technology**? .... and ....

Q4 EM waves with higher frequencies are generally more damaging. Explain, in terms of wavelength and frequency, why some **ultraviolet** radiation can be almost as damaging as **X-rays**.

....

....

Q5 **Radio** and **optical fibres** are two different ways of sending signals over long distances. Give two advantages and one disadvantage of using optical fibres compared to radio to send information.

Advantages: 1. ....

2. ....

Disadvantage: ....

Communicating with Light

Q1 Choose from the words below to complete the passage.

| pulses | thousands | reflected | internal | dense | core | infrared | multiplexing |

Optical fibres depend upon total .... reflection for their operation.

Visible light or .... waves are sent down the cable and are ....

when they hit the boundary between the .... fibre and the less ....

outer layer. The signals travel as .... of light. Each cable can carry

.... of different signals. This is called ....

Q2 Tick to show whether these statements are **true** or **false**. **True False**

a) Optical fibres carry pulses of light or infrared radiation. ☐ ☐

b) Optical fibres work because the light signal is refracted along the fibre. ☐ ☐

c) For the signal to be transmitted, the rays must not enter the fibre at too sharp an angle. ☐ ☐

d) Optical fibre signals are subject to lots of interference from other signals. ☐ ☐

Q3 **Morse code** was historically used to communicate over long distances using light signals.

Explain why Morse code is described as a digital signal.

....

....

Q4 **Optical fibres** can be used to supply **broadband internet**.

a) Give two advantages of using optical fibres for this purpose.

1. ....

2. ....

b) Name another common use of optical fibres.

....

Top Tips: Visible light is the EM wave we're most familiar with, so it's easy to take it for granted. Even before all the modern communications technology was invented, people were using light in a simple but effective way to communicate over long distances — although flashing a light on and off isn't **quite** as convenient as a quick text to tell your mum you'll be home for tea.

Lasers

Q1 The diagram shows how a **CD player** changes the pits on a CD into a signal which can be played through a loudspeaker.

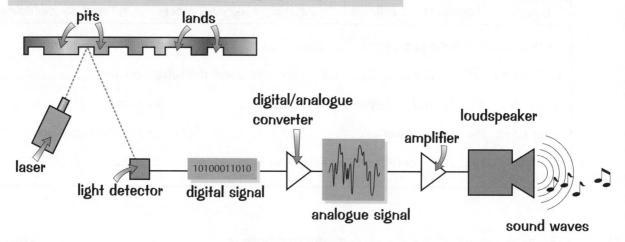

a) Why does the CD surface need to be **shiny**? ....

b) What happens to the laser light when it hits the **pit**?

....

c) How does the light sensor pick up the difference between **digital on**s **and off**s?

....

....

Q2 Circle the correct words to complete each of the sentences below.

a) Lasers produce a beam of **light** / **X-rays** in which all the waves have the same **frequency** / **pitch**.

b) The waves in a laser beam are all **in phase** / **out of phase** with each other, so the beam is said to be **divergent** / **coherent**.

c) The beam produced by a laser is **weak** / **intense** because the waves are **in phase** / **out of phase**.

Q3 A tour guide uses a small laser to point out things of interest high up on the walls of a cave.

a) Explain which property of lasers makes them useful for this purpose.

....

....

b) The laser pointer is **monochromatic**.
Explain why laser beams are monochromatic.

....

....

Infrared

Q1 Infrared radiation is used in **remote controls** for electrical devices.

a) Complete the paragraph below, choosing from the words in the box.

pattern	analogue	digital	bend	long	pulses	short	programmed	decode

A remote controls emits .... of infrared which form a

.... signal to control an electrical device such as a TV. The device will

detect and .... the pattern of pulses. E.g. a DVD player may be

.... to know that a certain .... of pulses means stop.

A remote control must be pointed straight at a device, because the waves do not

................................, and it won't work over .... distances because the

infrared beam is fairly weak.

b) Write down one other use of infrared radiation in communications.

....

Q2 Tick the boxes to show whether these statements are **true** or **false**.

		True	False
a)	Infrared radiation can be used for wireless communication.	☐	☐
b)	Infrared is too dangerous to be used in the home.	☐	☐
c)	Infrared radiation is known as heat radiation.	☐	☐
d)	Cold objects emit more infrared radiation than hot objects.	☐	☐
e)	Infrared radiation can be used to cook food.	☐	☐

Q3 All **hot objects** give out infrared radiation.

Describe **one** use of infrared that relies on this property.

....

....

Top Tips: The prefix 'infra' comes from Latin. It basically means 'below' — so infrared radiation is just radiation with a frequency below that of red light. The opposite of 'infra' is 'ultra', which means above or beyond — so ultraviolet radiation is just...   You get the idea...

Module P1 — Energy for the Home

Wireless Communication — Radio Waves

Q1 a) Only some of these statements are true. Circle their letters.

A Long waves such as radio waves are good for transmitting information long distances.

B Some wavelengths of radio wave are refracted by the ionosphere and come back to Earth.

C When a wave meets a medium with a different density it can change direction.
This is known as interference.

b) Write out a correct version of any false statements.

....

....

Q2 The house shown below receives radio signals from a nearby transmitter, even though there is a mountain between the house and the transmitter.

radio transmitter

Use the words below to fill in the blanks in the passage.

ionosphere   diffraction   short-wave   long-wave   refraction   absorbs   reflects   interference

The house can receive .... signals because they can bend around the

mountain. This is known as .... It also receives ....

signals because they are reflected by the ....

This is caused by .... of the radio waves as they change speed.

Q3 Draw arrows to **match up** the sentences.

Diffraction past an obstacle...

...can result in signal loss because the waves are spread out.

Refraction can disrupt a signal because it...

...means that some waves are not blocked by tall buildings.

Diffraction at transmission dishes...

...can bend waves away from receiver dishes.

Wireless Communication — Radio Waves

Q4 Fill in the gaps in this passage using the words below.

reflected   quickly   reflection   long   ionosphere   slowly   ionises   refraction   diffraction

Ultraviolet radiation from the Sun .... some of the atoms high in the atmosphere,

forming a layer known as the .... When a radio wave with a short wavelength

meets this layer of charged particles it travels more .... and its direction is changed.

This is known as .... The radio wave is .... back to Earth.

Q5 The diagram shows two different radio waves **A** and **B** being transmitted and received from **radio masts** on the Earth. Both waves have the same frequency.

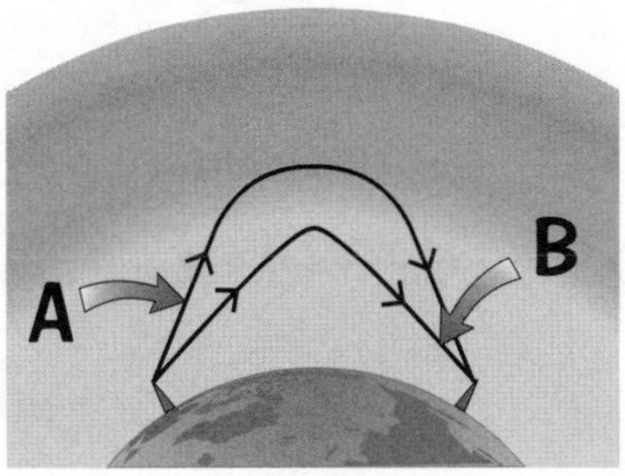

a) Which of the waves is transmitted at a **higher angle of elevation**?

....

b) What effect does the **angle of elevation** have on the **speed** at which information is received at the second mast?

....

....

Q6 Wendy listens to a radio talk show on a **digital radio** in her lounge. She then goes out into the garden and listens to the same radio talk show on a **portable analogue radio**.

a) The voices of the radio talk show host and their guests sound much **clearer** on the **digital** radio than they do on the analogue radio. Explain why this is.

....

....

....

b) Radio stations use **multiplexing** to digitally broadcast their radio signals. Explain what 'multiplexing' means.

....

....

c) Give one disadvantage of digital audio broadcasting.

....

Wireless Communication — Microwaves

Q1   Tick to show which of the following statements are **true**.
Write out a correct version of any false statements.   **True**

a)   Microwave signals can be affected by adverse weather.   ☐

b)   Microwaves can diffract around large obstacles such as a large block of flats.   ☐

c)   Microwaves used for communication are all absorbed by
the watery atmosphere before they can reach a satellite.   ☐

d)   Long wavelength waves are diffracted more than short ones.   ☐

....

....

....

Q2   Gabrielle in London and Carwyn in Toronto are talking by **mobile phone**.

NOT TO SCALE   Communications
Satellite

Carwyn's
phone

Gabrielle's
phone

Atlantic Ocean

Think about what
microwaves can
and can't do.

a)   Gabrielle's mobile phone sends a signal to a **transmitter**. The transmitter sends a signal to the
communications satellite. Why **doesn't** Gabrielle's phone send the signal **straight to Carwyn's**?

....

b)   Carwyn goes into the centre of Toronto, and finds that her mobile phone sometimes **loses
reception** when she walks down streets with a lot of **tall buildings**. Explain why this happens.

....

....

Q3   Mobile phones emit microwaves when you are making a call.

Explain why this could be a potential health risk.

....

....

....

EM Receivers

Q1   **Radio telescopes** need to be very large, or else the images are 'fuzzy' and lack detail.

a) Compete the paragraph below to explain why, choosing from the words in the box.

size	wavelength	reflected	little	diffracted	detail	gap	lots of	receiver	large

When a wave enters a .... it passes through a gap and gets

.... (spread out) so some .... is lost.

The amount of diffraction is affected by the .... of the gap

compared to the size of the .... of the wave. A gap about the

same size as the wavelength causes .... diffraction.

So to get lots of detail you need the receiver to be as .... as possible.

b) To produce images with a similar degree of detail, which would need to be **larger** — an infrared telescope or a microwave telescope? Circle the correct answer.

infrared   **microwave**

c) Explain your answer to part **b)**.

    ....

    ....

d) Explain why optical telescopes can be a lot smaller than radio telescopes.

    ....

    ....

Q2   The **resolution** of an optical **microscope** is limited because of **diffraction**.

Explain why this is.

    ....

    ....

    ....

Top Tips: With telescopes, the rule seems to be 'big is beautiful'. And it's best to think up a good name to make sure everyone knows your telescope's the biggest. There's one in Chile called the Very Large Telescope. Imaginative. Better still, there are plans to build a really big new optical telescope — 100 m across — and call it the Overwhelmingly Large Telescope. Beat that.

Analogue and Digital Signals

Q1 Describe the main difference between **digital** and **analogue** signals.

....

....

Q2 Sketch: a 'clean' digital signal.   a 'noisy' digital signal.   a 'noisy' analogue signal.

Q3 Fill in the blanks, using the words below.

analogue	digital	refract	amplified	weaken	interference	noise

All signals .... as they travel. To overcome this, they can be

.... Signals may also suffer .... from other

signals or from electrical disturbances. This causes .... in the signal.

When .... signals are amplified, the noise is also amplified.

Q4 Digital signals have many advantages over analogue signals.

a) Explain why digital signals suffer less from **noise** than analogue signals.

....

....

b) Describe one other advantage of using digital signals for communication.

....

....

Humans and the Environment

Q1 Prolonged exposure to the Sun is linked to an increased risk of **skin cancer**.

a) Which part of the radiation from the Sun causes the damage? ....

b) How are human cells affected by this radiation?

....

Q2 Marie has **darker skin** than her friend, so she has slightly more protection from harmful radiation.

a) **How** does darker skin give this protection?

....

....

b) Suggest two ways you can **reduce** your exposure to harmful radiation from the Sun.

1. ....

2. ....

c) Marie uses a sun cream with '**SPF 25**' on the label. What does 'SPF 25' mean?

....

Q3 The **ozone layer** helps protect life on Earth.

a) Where is the ozone layer? ....

b) How does the ozone layer help protect life on Earth?

....

c) Name one group of pollutant gases which break up ozone molecules.

....

Q4 Scientists discovered a '**hole**' in the ozone layer over **Antarctica**.

a) How do scientists verify their findings?

....

....

b) Describe one way that the international community responded to the discovery of the 'hole'.

....

Seismic Waves

Q1 The diagram shows four layers of the Earth. Complete the table.

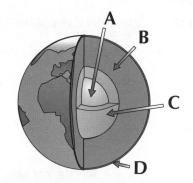

Layer	Solid or Liquid	Which seismic waves (S, P or both) can travel through the layer?
A		
B		
C		
D		

Q2 Read the following sentences and underline the correct word from each highlighted pair.

Disturbances in the Earth produce **EM** / **seismic** waves which can travel **through** / **along** the Earth. These waves can be recorded on a **seismograph** / **thermogram**.

Q3 Earthquakes can produce both **S waves** and **P waves**.

a) Which of these two types are **longitudinal** waves? ....

b) Which of these two types travels **faster**? ....

c) Which type of wave **cannot** travel through the **outer core** of the Earth? ....

Q4 Circle the letters next to any of these statements which are **true**.

A Both P and S waves can travel from the North Pole to the South Pole.

B A longitudinal wave travels in the same direction as the force which causes it.

C Transverse waves travel at right angles to the force which causes them.

D P waves travel more slowly through the inner core. This suggests that it is made of solid material.

Q5 Both P and S waves **curve** as they travel through the Earth.

a) Why do they curve?

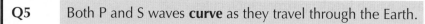

b) P waves can change direction abruptly as they travel through the Earth. Explain why this happens.

....

c) **i)** Which type of wave doesn't reach the opposite point of the Earth to the site of an earthquake?

....

ii) What does this tell seismologists about the structure of the Earth's interior?

....

Mixed Questions — Module P1

Q1 Infrared radiation is used by TV **remote controls**. Jake shows Peter that he can change the TV channel by pointing the remote control at a mirror on the opposite wall.

a) What property of EM rays has Jake demonstrated? Circle the correct answer.

  reflection   **refraction**   **diffraction**

b) Peter places a dull black piece of card over the mirror and tries to change channel in the same way. Explain what will happen now and why.

....

....

Q2 Steve has bought a new fridge-freezer.

a) Steve's new fridge-freezer has its freezer compartment above the refrigerator.
How does this arrangement encourage **convection currents** in the main body of the fridge?

....

....

b) Most fridges have a light which comes on when the door is opened. The light in Steve's new fridge wastes 68 J of energy for every 100 J of useful output energy. Calculate the light's efficiency.

....

....

Q3 My landline telephone is connected to the telephone exchange by **optical fibres**.

a) What **type** of EM wave might be sent from the exchange? ....

b) Draw an annotated diagram to
show how an optical fibre works.

Mixed Questions — Module P1

Q4   Erik investigates ways of saving energy in his grandma's house. He calculates the annual savings that could be made on his grandma's fuel bills, and the cost of doing the work.

Work needed	Annual Saving (£)	Cost of work (£)
Hot water tank jacket	20	20
Draught-proofing	70	80
Cavity wall insulation	85	650
Thermostatic controls	30	140

a)   Which of the options in the table would save Erik's grandma the most money **over 5 years**? Show your working.

....

....

b)   Erik's grandma likes to have a hot bath in the evenings. How much energy is needed to heat 90 kg of water from 14 °C to 36 °C ? (The specific heat capacity of water is 4200 J/kg/°C.)

....

....

c)   Erik goes on an Arctic expedition. He has to melt snow for drinking water. What mass of snow (at 0 °C) could he melt using the same amount of energy his grandma uses to heat her bath water? (The specific latent heat of water for melting is 334 000 J/kg.)

....

....

Q5   The diagram below shows the paths of some seismic waves travelling through the Earth.

a)   Label the layers **i)** to **iv)** on the diagram as solid or liquid.

b)   All the waves whose paths are shown are of the same type. What type are they? Circle the correct answer.

       P waves   **S waves**

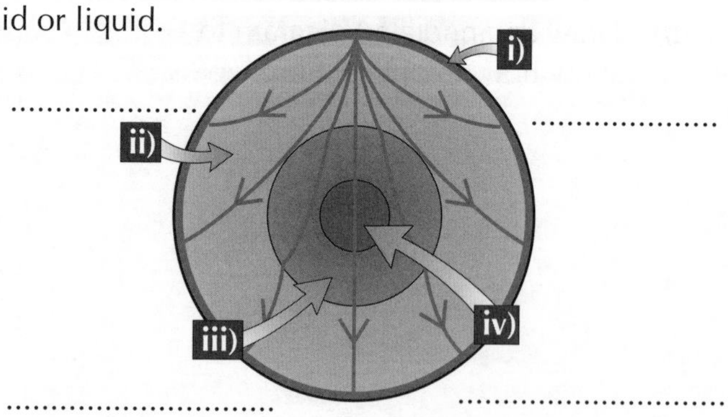

c)   The waves curve gradually in layer **ii)** but change direction suddenly at the boundary between layers **ii)** and **iii)**. Explain why.

....

....

Mixed Questions — Module P1

Q6 Waves A, B and C represent **infrared**, **visible light** and **ultraviolet** radiation (not in that order). They are all drawn to the same scale.

a) Which of the waves has the greatest amplitude? ....

b) Which of the waves represents UV radiation? ....

c) Describe one way in which human activities have caused an increase in our exposure to UV radiation from sunlight.

....

....

Q7 Radio Roary transmits **long-wave** signals with a wavelength of **1.5 km**.

a) Calculate the **frequency** of Radio Roary's transmission. (Use speed = 3 × 10⁸ m/s.)

....

....

b) Mr Potts is on holiday in the Scottish Highlands. The cottage he's staying in has a TV and radio. Mr Potts has a favourite show on a short-wave radio station, but finds that he can only get long-wave radio reception. TV reception is also very poor, so he can't watch his favourite cookery and gardening shows.

Explain why Mr Potts gets **good** long-wave radio reception, but such **poor** short-wave radio and TV reception.

....

....

c) Radio Piracy broadcasts at a frequency of 201 kHz. Both Radio Roary and Radio Piracy broadcast **analogue** signals.

i) Why might Radio Piracy's frequency be a problem for people listening to these stations?

....

ii) Suggest a way to reduce the problem without changing the frequency of the transmissions.

....

d) Mr Potts' holiday cottage has a microwave oven. The microwaves used in ovens are different from those used to carry mobile phone signals. Explain how they differ, and why different types are used.

....

....

Classification

Q1 a) Organisms can be **classified** into different groups. Fill in the missing labels on the diagram to show the names of the different groups.

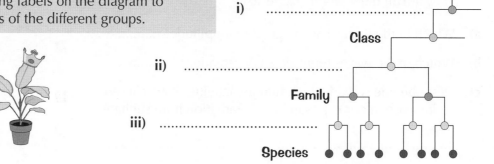

i) ....

ii) ....

iii) ....

b) Describe the difference between **natural** and **artificial** classification systems.

....

....

c) Explain why it can be difficult to classify living organisms into distinct groups.

....

Q2 Complete the following passage to explain why **classification systems change** over time. The words you need are in the box below.

genetic	classification	sequencing	species	adapted	related

Sometimes when a new .... is discovered it doesn't really fit into any of

the groups in the existing .... system. As a result, the system has to be

.... to include the new species. DNA .... of species

that we already know lots about can show us .... differences between

different groups. This data might change our minds about how closely ....

two groups of organisms are — causing us to change how we classify them.

Q3 Use the information in the passage to **label** the **evolutionary tree** below with the letters A-D.

A and B are fossilised bones from the legs of ancestors of the modern horse. Some scientists believe that animals with legs like fossil A gradually developed into animals with legs like fossil B. It is thought that there was a stage in the development of the horse between A and B, during which the leg bone would have looked like C. Animals with legs like fossil D are closely related to animals with legs like fossil B. But, those animals with legs like fossil D aren't direct ancestors of the modern horse.

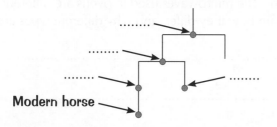

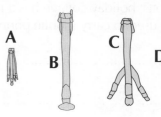

Species

Q1 **Species** are named using the **binomial system**.

a) Give a definition for the term '**species**'.

....

....

b) What exactly does **binomial** mean?

....

c) The binomial name for humans is *Homo sapiens*.
Which part of the name refers to the species that humans belong to?

....

Q2 Donkeys and horses are different **species**. When a donkey and a horse reproduce the resulting offspring is a **mule**. Give **one** problem with classifying hybrid organisms like the mule into species.

Hee Haaawwwww

....

....

Q3 Dave thinks he's discovered a new species of bacterium, but he isn't sure. Bacteria **reproduce asexually**. Explain why this makes it difficult to classify bacteria into species.

....

....

Q4 a) Explain how comparing the **common ancestors** of two species can tell us how **closely related** the species are.

....

....

b) **Llamas** and **camels** are closely related, but they look very different.
Explain why this might be the case.

....

....

<u>Pyramids of Biomass and Numbers</u>

Q1 The following diagram shows a garden food chain. The **number** and **dry biomass** of the organisms at each stage in the food chain is shown below.

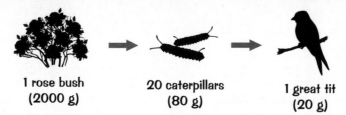

1 rose bush   20 caterpillars   1 great tit
(2000 g)   (80 g)   (20 g)

a) Draw and label a **pyramid of biomass** for the food chain in the grid below. Each **large** square of the grid should represent **200 grams**.

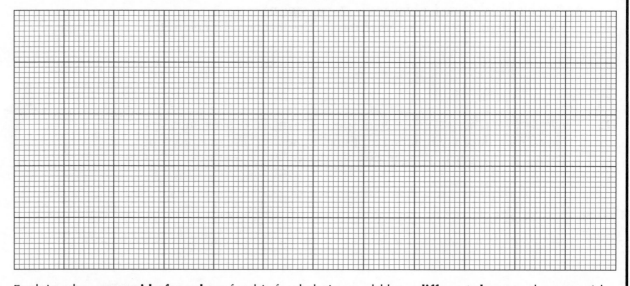

b) Explain why a **pyramid of numbers** for this food chain would be a **different shape** to the pyramid of biomass you've drawn above.

....

....

Q2 Drawing pyramids of biomass is not always straightforward.

a) To construct a pyramid of biomass, you have to measure the **dry biomass** of the organisms in a food chain.

   i) What is dry biomass?

....

   ii) Give **one** reason why measuring dry biomass can be difficult.

....

b) Give **one** other reason why it can be difficult to construct pyramids of biomass.

....

....

Energy Transfer and Energy Flow

Q1   Complete the sentences below by circling the correct words.

a)   Nearly all life on Earth depends on **food** / **energy** from the Sun.

b)   **Plants** / **Animals** can make their own food by a process called **photosynthesis** / **respiration**.

c)   To obtain energy animals must **decay** / **eat** plant material or other animals.

d)   Animals and plants release energy through the process of **photosynthesis** / **respiration**.

e)   Some of the energy released in animals is **gained** / **lost** as **growth** / **heat**
before it reaches organisms at later steps of the food chain.

Q2   A **food chain** is shown in the diagram.

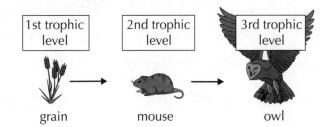

a)   Put the following amounts of energy
under the correct organisms.

500 kJ,   50 000 kJ,   8000 kJ

b)   Calculate the amount of energy lost between the:

i)   1st and 2nd trophic levels. ....

ii)   2nd and 3rd trophic levels. ....

c)   Calculate the efficiency of energy transfer from the:

i)   1st to 2nd trophic level. ....

ii)   2nd to 3rd trophic level. ....

Q3   Study the diagram of **energy transfer** shown.

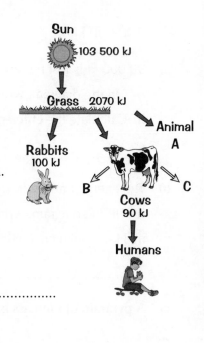

a)   Using the figures shown on the diagram, work out the
percentage of the Sun's energy that is available in the grass.

    ....

b)   The efficiency of energy transfer from the grass to the next trophic
level is 10%. Work out how much energy is available in animal A.

    ....

c)   **B** and **C** are processes that represent energy loss.
Suggest what these processes might be.

    ....

d)   Why do food chains rarely have more than five trophic levels?

    ....

    ....

Energy Transfer and Energy Flow

Q4   Another **food chain** is shown below.

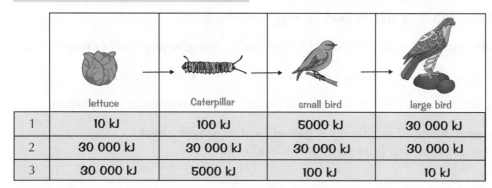

leaf it out

	lettuce	Caterpillar	small bird	large bird
1	10 kJ	100 kJ	5000 kJ	30 000 kJ
2	30 000 kJ	30 000 kJ	30 000 kJ	30 000 kJ
3	30 000 kJ	5000 kJ	100 kJ	10 kJ

a)   Which row, 1, 2 or 3, shows the amount of energy available at each trophic level? ....

b)   Circle the answer below that shows how much energy is available to the caterpillar.

| 5000 kJ | | 25 000 kJ | | 30 000 kJ |

c)   Circle the answer below that shows how much energy is lost from the caterpillar to the small bird.

| 100 kJ | | 4900 kJ | | 5000 kJ |

Q5   An **aquatic food chain** is shown.

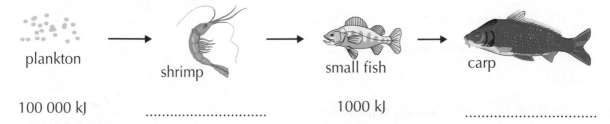

plankton

shrimp

small fish

carp

100 000 kJ   ....   1000 kJ   ....

a)   90 000 kJ is lost between the 1st trophic level (plankton) and the 2nd trophic level (shrimp).

   i)   On the diagram, write the amount of energy available in the shrimp for the small fish.

   ii) Calculate the **efficiency** of energy transfer from the 1st to the 2nd trophic level.

   ....

b)   The energy transfer from the small fish to the carp is **5%** efficient.

   i)   On the diagram, write the amount of **energy** available in the **carp**.

   ii) How much energy is **lost** from the food chain at this stage?

   ....

c)   A **pyramid of biomass** is drawn for this food chain. Explain why it is pyramid shaped.

   ....

   ....

Interactions Between Organisms

Q1   **Similar organisms** living in the same habitat are often in **close competition** for resources.

a)   Explain why this is the case.

....

b)   Complete the sentences about competition below by circling the correct word in each pair.

i)   **Intraspecific** / **Interspecific** competition is where organisms compete for resources against individuals of another species.

ii) **Intraspecific** / **Interspecific** competition is where organisms compete for resources against individuals of the same species.

iii) Intraspecific competition often has a **smaller** / **bigger** impact on organisms than interspecific competition.

Q2   Explain what is meant by the term '**ecological niche**'.

....

....

Q3   Look at the **population graph** for the heron and frog.

a)   Which animal is the **predator** and which is the **prey**?

Predator: ....   Prey: ....

b)   Shortly after an increase in the number of herons, what happens to the number of frogs?

....

c)   Name two factors that will **reduce** the frog population.

1. ....   2. ....

d)   If the frogs run out of food, what will happen to the number of herons?

....

e)   Explain why predator-prey population cycles are always out of phase with each other.

....

....

Interactions Between Organisms

Q4   Some organisms, such as **parasites**, depend entirely on other species for their survival.

a)   **Two** of the organisms below are parasites. Circle the correct two.

| Flea | Tapeworm | Tiddles | Bumble bee |

b)   What is the difference between a **parasitic** relationship and **mutualism**?

....

....

c)   **i)**   State one example of **mutualism**. ....

ii) Explain why your answer to part **i)** is an example of mutualism.

....

....

iii) Suggest how the **interdependence** of the species in your
answer to part **i)** could affect their **abundance**.

....

....

Q5   Read the passage below and answer the questions that follow.

> Barn owls compete with each other for mates, hunting territories, nesting
> sites and food. Foxes and barn owls feed on many of the same species of
> small mammal. They compete with each other for food, but nothing else.

a)   Is the competition between **foxes** and **barn owls** intraspecific or interspecific?

....

b)   Which type of competition will have a **bigger impact** on the **barn owl population**?

....

c)   Explain your answer to part **b)**.

....

....

Adaptations

Q1 Animals and plants are **adapted** to their environments.

a) Explain what is meant by the term '**adaptation**'.

....

....

b) Explain why animals and plants need to adapt to their environment.

....

....

Q2 Complete these sentences by inserting the word '**generalists**' or '**specialists**' into the gaps.

a) .... are highly adapted to survive in a specific habitat.

b) .... are adapted to survive in a range of different habitats.

c) In a habitat with stable conditions .... will out compete ....

d) In a habitat with changing conditions .... will out compete ....

Q3 a) Complete the paragraph about organisms that are adapted to live in **extreme conditions** using some of the words in the box below.

extremophobes	enzymes	optimum	optical	extremophiles	denature

Some organisms are adapted to survive in extreme conditions. Organisms that are adapted

to survive in the most extreme conditions are called .... For example,

bacteria that live in extremely hot environments have .... with very high

.... temperatures. These temperatures would ....

the enzymes of most other organisms.

b) Organisms that live in extremely **cold environments** often produce special '**antifreeze proteins**'. What are 'antifreeze proteins'?

....

....

Module B2 — Understanding Our Environment

Adaptations to Cold Environments

Q1 **Fur seals** are adapted to survive in **very cold conditions**.

a) Apart from having a thick furry coat, suggest **one** other anatomical adaptation that might insulate the fur seal's body and trap heat in.

....

b) Fur seals have a **large size** and a **compact body shape**. Does this give them a small or a large **surface area to volume ratio**? Tick the box next to the correct answer below.

small surface area to volume ratio ☐   large surface area to volume ratio ☐

c) Explain how their surface area to volume ratio helps fur seals survive in cold conditions.

....

....

Q2 The diagram shows a **counter-current heat exchange system** in the leg of a seagull.

a) Explain how the counter-current heat exchange system reduces the amount of heat that the seagull loses to the environment.

....

....

....

....

....

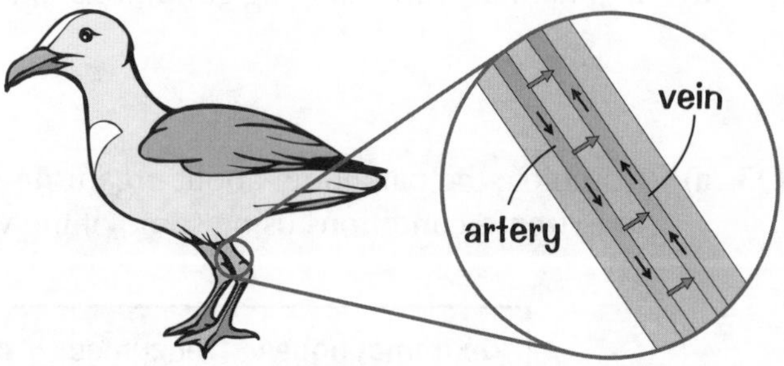

b) Name **one** other organism that has a counter-current heat exchange system.

....

Q3 **Hibernation** is a behavioural adaptation to **cold environments**.
Explain how hibernation helps animals in cold environments to **survive**.

....

....

....

Adaptations to Hot and Dry Environments

Q1   Complete the sentences below about **adaptations to hot environments** by circling the correct word(s) from each pair.

a) To keep cool in warm environments, organisms need to **increase / reduce** heat gain and **increase / reduce** heat loss.

b) Being active at night is **a behavioural / an anatomical** adaptation to living in a hot climate.

c) Some animals spend the day in the shade or underground to reduce the amount of heat their bodies **gain from / lose to** their surroundings.

d) Having a **small / large** surface area to volume ratio helps an animal to lose heat to its surroundings.

Q2   Margaret is looking at some photos of **elephants** that her uncle took on a trip to South Africa.

Margaret asks her biology teacher why the elephants' ears are so large.

Her teacher says that the elephants' large ears are an adaptation which helps them to **lose heat**.

Suggest how having large ears could help elephants to lose heat.

....

....

Q3   Desert animals and plants are well adapted to living in **dry conditions**.

a) Give **one** adaptation that helps **animals** to survive in dry environments.

....

b) i) Give **one** adaptation that helps **plants** to survive in dry environments.

....

ii) Explain how your answer to part **i)** helps the plants to survive.

....

....

Top Tips: Whenever you're thinking about adaptations to dry environments, all you need to think about is water — organisms need to get as much (and lose as little) of it as they can.

Evolution and Speciation

Q1   Giraffes used to have much **shorter** necks than they do today.

The statements below give an explanation, according to Darwin's theory, of how their neck length changed. Write numbers in the boxes to show the **order** the statements should be in.

☐ The giraffes competed for food from low branches. This food started to become scarce. Many giraffes died before they could breed.

☐ More long-necked giraffes survived to breed, so more giraffes were born with long necks.

☐ A giraffe was born with a longer neck than normal. The long-necked giraffe was able to eat more food.

☐ All giraffes had short necks.

☐ The long-necked giraffe survived to have lots of offspring that all had longer necks.

☐ All giraffes have long necks.

Q2   Darwin's theory of natural selection wasn't perfect. Use the words in the box below to complete the paragraph explaining how Darwin's theory was **developed**.

DNA	appeared	inherit	Successful	offspring

Darwin's theory couldn't explain why new characteristics .... or

how beneficial adaptations were passed from parents to their ....

We now know that adaptations are controlled by an organism's ....

.... adaptations are passed on to offspring in the genes that they

.... from their parents.

Q3   The development of new species is called **speciation**.
Speciation requires **reproductive isolation**.

a)   What is 'reproductive isolation'?

....

b)   Explain how the **geographic isolation** of two populations can lead to reproductive isolation.

....

....

....

....

Theories of Evolution

Q1 **Lamarck** had a different theory of evolution to Darwin.

a) What was Lamarck's theory of evolution?

....

....

....

b) Explain why Lamarck's ideas were rejected.

....

....

....

Q2 Darwin knew that his theory would stir up some **trouble**, so he didn't publish his work for a long time.

a) Which group of people were particularly upset about Darwin's theory of natural selection?

....

b) Explain why these people were offended by Darwin's theory.

....

....

Q3 Darwin's theory of natural selection is now **widely accepted** as the best explanation of evolution.

Give two reasons why this is the case.

1. ....

....

2. ....

....

Top Tips: You might've thought that all this stuff about Darwin upsetting people was just a bit of background information, but it could come up in the exam — so make sure you don't skip through it when you're revising. It's just as important as understanding what Darwin's theory actually was.

The Carbon Cycle and Decomposition

Q1 Follow the instructions below to complete the diagram of part of the **carbon cycle**.

a) Add an arrow or arrows labelled **P** to represent **photosynthesis**.

b) Add an arrow or arrows labelled **R** to represent **respiration**.

c) Add an arrow or arrows labelled **F** to represent **feeding**.

| CO₂ in the air |

| plant | | animal |

Q2 **Carbon** is a very important element that is constantly being recycled.

a) What is the one way that carbon is removed from the atmosphere?

....

b) In what form is carbon removed from the atmosphere?

....

c) What is this carbon converted into by plants?

....

d) How is this carbon passed on through the food chain?

....

....

e) By what process do **all** living organisms return carbon to the air?

....

Q3 The **rate** at which carbon is recycled depends on the **conditions** in the soil.

a) i) How would the rate of carbon recycling be different in a **waterlogged** soil, compared to a **well-drained** soil?

....

ii) Explain your answer to part **i)**.

....

....

....

b) Explain why the **acidity** of the soil would also affect the rate of recycling.

....

....

The Carbon Cycle and Decomposition

Q4 Carbon can also be recycled in the **oceans**. Complete the paragraph below about carbon in the oceans using some of the words from the box.

carbon dioxide	water	carbon sinks	granite	atmosphere	limestone
storms	carbonates	rocks	volcanic eruptions		carbon houses

The oceans absorb huge volumes of .... They act as massive stores

of carbon called .... Many species of marine organisms also store

carbon in shells made out of .... When the organisms die,

these shells fall to the ocean floor. Over a long period of time, the shells slowly form

.... rocks. After weathering or .... , the carbon

from these rocks is released back into the ....

Q5 The diagram below shows a version of the **carbon cycle**.

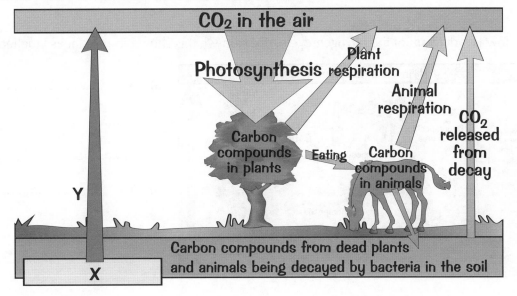

a) Name substance **X** shown on the diagram above. ....

b) Explain why substance **X** contains carbon.

....

....

c) Name the process labelled **Y** on the diagram above. ....

Top Tips: Carbon's super important. Thankfully all that carbon we release from respiration is recycled when plants photosynthesise. They take in the carbon and use it again to make fats, proteins and carbohydrates — which then get passed along the food chain to us. Make sure you can do all the questions on these pages before your exam — the carbon cycle's a favourite topic for examiners.

The Nitrogen Cycle

Q1 Match up each type of **organism** below with the way it obtains **nitrogen**.

Plants — By breaking down dead organisms and animal waste

Animals — By absorbing nitrates from the soil

Decomposers — By eating other organisms

Q2 The nitrogen cycle is dependent on a number of different types of **bacteria**. Explain the role of each of the following types of bacteria in the nitrogen cycle.

Type of bacteria | **Role in the nitrogen cycle**

a) Decomposers ....

b) Nitrifying bacteria ....

c) Denitrifying bacteria ....

d) Nitrogen-fixing bacteria ....

Q3 Below is a diagram of the **nitrogen cycle**. Explain what is shown in the stages labelled:

a) X ....

....

....

b) Y ....

....

....

Q4 A farmer was told that if he planted **legume plants** his soil would become more **fertile**.

a) Explain how the legume plants would increase the fertility of his soil.

....

....

b) Explain how this would improve plant growth.

....

....

Module B2 — Understanding Our Environment

Human Impact on the Environment

Q1   **Pollution** from human activities has been shown to cause lots of problems for the environment.

a)   Give **one** cause of acid rain.

....

b)   Suggest **one** consequence of global warming.

....

c)   Define the term '**carbon footprint**'.

....

....

Q2   Complete the passage by choosing the correct words from the list below.

Some words can be used more than once.

exponentially	slowly	more	developed	higher	lower
poor	less	pollution	resources	environment	population	developing

Populations increase when birth rate is .... than death rate. The world's

population is increasing .... This means there is ....

pressure on the .... We're using up .... and causing

.... This is especially true of .... countries who demand a

.... standard of living. These countries cause the most ....,

but have a relatively small proportion of the world's ....

Q3   In 1985, scientists discovered a **hole** in the **ozone layer** above Antarctica.

a)   What caused the hole in the ozone layer?

....

....

b)   Suggest why scientists studying the hole above Antarctica today
should wear sunscreen if they are working outdoors.

....

c)   Suggest **one** other possible consequence of the hole in the ozone layer.

....

....

Human Impact on the Environment

Q4   Mayfly larvae and sludgeworms can be studied to see how much **sewage** is in water.

a)   What is the name for an organism used in this way? ....

Juanita recorded the number of each species in water samples taken at three different distances away from a sewage outlet. Her results are shown below.

Distance (km)	No. of mayfly larvae	No. of sludgeworms
1	3	20
2	11	14
3	23	7

b)   What can you conclude about the two organisms from these results?

....

....

Q5   Dave is investigating the local air quality. He collects data on the **sulfur dioxide concentration** in the air at different sites in his town. His data is shown in the table below.

Site	sulfur dioxide concentration (micrograms/m^3)
1	9.8
2	9.4
3	7.1

a)   At which site is the sulfur dioxide concentration the **highest**?

....

b)   Dave measured the sulfur dioxide concentration directly, using specialist equipment.
Give one advantage and one disadvantage of using **non-living methods** to measure pollution.

Advantage: ....

Disadvantage: ....

c)   i) Give an example of an **indicator species** that could be used to monitor **air quality**.

....

ii) Suggest **one** reason why Dave did not use indicator species in his study.

....

....

Endangered Species

Q1 Fill in the gaps, choosing from the words below. You might not need all the words.

restrictions ensuring medicines conservation

undiscovered television endangered plants extinct

.... programmes often benefit much more than the ....

species they are designed for. One example is the .... put in place on fishing.

By stopping people from over-fishing areas, we are .... the future supply of

fish stocks. Another example is the conservation of rainforests. Many of the medicines that we

use today come from .... If the rainforests are not protected, undiscovered

species may become .... and we could miss out on valuable medicines.

Q2 The mountain gorilla is an **endangered** species threatened with **extinction**.

a) What is **extinction**?

....

....

b) Suggest why the **number of available habitats** might be an important
factor in determining whether or not gorillas become extinct.

....

....

You don't need to know about gorillas specifically — think about how animals in general become extinct.

Q3 **Conservation programmes** are designed to protect endangered species. Explain why each
of the following factors should be considered when evaluating conservation programmes:

a) interaction between species.

....

....

b) viability of populations.

....

....

Sustainable Development

Q1 a) Give a definition for the term **sustainable development**.

....

b) The human population is increasing. Give two ways in which this makes sustainable development more difficult.

1. ....

....

2. ....

....

Q2 Tick the right boxes to say whether the sentences below are **true** or **false**.

		True	False
a)	Sustainable development has no impact on endangered species.	☐	☐
b)	Whales still have commercial value when they are dead.	☐	☐
c)	It's legal to kill whales for scientific research.	☐	☐
d)	It's easy to keep track of how many whales are killed by different countries.	☐	☐
e)	Scientists understand exactly how whales communicate.	☐	☐
f)	Keeping whales in captivity is not useful for scientists.	☐	☐

Q3 Describe how **fishing** has changed to become more sustainable.

....

....

Q4 Explain the role that **education** can play in sustainable development.

....

....

Top Tips: Sustainable development is a hot topic. It's not just important for your exam — it's also important in the real world. Which is a pretty good reason to make sure you learn about it really.

Mixed Questions — Module B2

Q1 a) The following statements describe how **speciation** can be caused by **geographic isolation**.

Write numbers in the boxes to show the **order** the statements should be in.

- ☐ Different mutations create different new features in the two groups of organisms.
- ☐ Eventually, the two populations will change so much that they become two separate, reproductively isolated species.
- ☐ A physical barrier divides a population of a species, e.g. a river changes its course.
- ☐ Natural selection works on the features so that, if they are beneficial, they spread through each of the populations.

b) Geographic isolation can result in **small populations** with **low genetic variation**. Explain why a species with low genetic variation is at risk of **extinction**.

....

....

Q2 Read the passage below and answer the questions that follow.

> Red and grey squirrels are similar species and belong to the same genus. In Britain, red squirrels (_Sciurus vulgaris_) have become endangered because of competition from grey squirrels. Grey squirrels are generalists and are successful in different forest ecosystems. Red squirrels, on the other hand, are specialists.

a) Explain why **similar species**, like red and grey squirrels, are likely to **compete**.

....

b) Explain what is meant by the term '**generalist**'.

....

c) Fill in the missing word to complete the sentence below:

The grey squirrel's Latin name is .... _carolinensis._

Q3 Legumes have a **mutualistic** relationship with bacteria that live in their root nodules. The bacteria turn atmospheric nitrogen into nitrogen compounds that the plants can use.

a) What name is given to these bacteria? ....

b) What do plants need nitrogen for?

....

c) Explain why the relationship between bean plants and these bacteria is **mutualistic**.

....

....

Mixed Questions — Module B2

Q4 The diagram below shows a **food chain** observed on the savannahs of Tanzania. It also shows the amount of **energy** available in each trophic level.

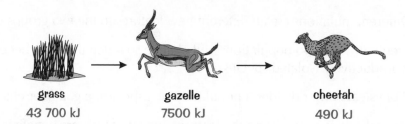

grass
43 700 kJ

gazelle
7500 kJ

cheetah
490 kJ

a) **i)** How much energy is lost from the 1st trophic level (grass) to the next (gazelle)?

....

ii) Calculate the efficiency of this energy transfer.

....

b) Suggest **two** ways in which energy might be lost by the gazelle.

....

....

c) Suggest how the waste products from this food chain could form the start of a new food chain.

....

....

d) **Carbon** also moves through the food chain. It is continuously being **recycled** from one form to another as the diagram below shows.

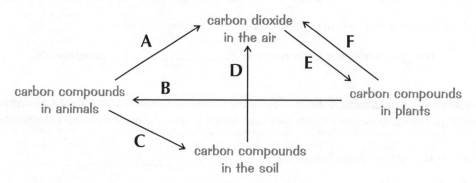

Name the processes labelled **A, B, C, D, E** and **F** in the diagram.

A ....   B ....

C ....   D ....

E ....   F ....

Mixed Questions — Module B2

Q5 Two types of **goose** found in the UK are the greylag goose and the white-fronted goose. The Latin name for the greylag goose is *Anser anser* and the white-fronted goose is *Anser albifrons*.

a) How can you tell that these two geese are different species?

....

b) How can you tell that the two species must be closely related?

....

c) **i)** What name is given to the system of identifying species by giving them two names?

....

ii) Explain why this system is used all over the world for naming species.

....

....

d) Explain why it's important to classify living organisms into groups such as species.

....

....

Q6 **Environmental pollution** is a major problem in some areas.

a) Magnus suspects that a paper factory down the road from his house is **polluting** a local river. Describe how Magnus could tell whether the river is polluted.

....

....

....

b) **i)** Suggest what the paper factory in Magnus's town might do to make the business more **sustainable**.

....

....

ii) Suggest how sustainable development can help **endangered species**.

....

....

....

The Earth's Structure

Q1   **Label** this simple diagram of the Earth's interior.

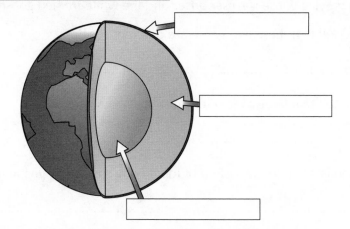

Q2   Draw a line to match up each key phrase or word to the correct description.

Lithosphere	The Earth's thin outer layer of solid rock.
Crust	Large pieces of the lithosphere.
Mantle	Caused by sudden movements of plates against each other.
Tectonic plates	The crust and upper mantle, made up of a 'jigsaw' of plates.
Seismic waves	A solid section of the Earth between the crust and the core.
Earthquake	Shock waves produced by an earthquake or an explosion.

Q3   Choose from the words in this list to complete the paragraph below.

solid   heat   tectonic   mantle   convection   crust   slow   radioactive   core   fast

.... decay in the mantle produces a lot of ...., which

causes .... currents to flow in the .... These currents

drive the movement of the Earth's .... plates. The movement of the

plates is very .... — they move at a rate of about 2.5 cm per year.

Q4   Complete the sentences below by circling the correct option from each pair.

a)   The Earth's crust is so **hot / thick** that you can't drill through it to study the Earth's structure directly.

b)   Instead, geologists use **seismic / electromagnetic** waves to study the inner structure of the Earth.

c)   P-waves can travel through solids and liquids. S-waves can only travel through **solids / liquids**.

d)   S-waves can't travel through the **mantle / outer core**, so we know that it must be **solid / liquid**.

The Earth's Structure

Q5 Look at the diagram showing the boundary between two tectonic plates.

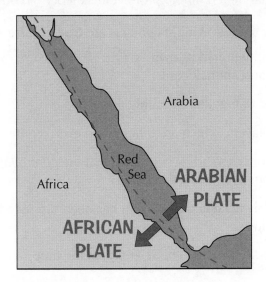

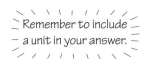

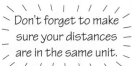

The Red Sea is widening at a speed of 1.6 cm per year.

a) If the sea level remains the same, how much will the Red Sea widen in 10 000 years?

....

Remember to include a unit in your answer.

b) The Red Sea is currently exactly 325 km wide at a certain point. If the sea level remains the same, how wide will the Red Sea be at this point in 20 000 years' time?

....

....

Don't forget to make sure your distances are in the same unit.

Q6 The map below on the left shows where most of the world's earthquakes take place.

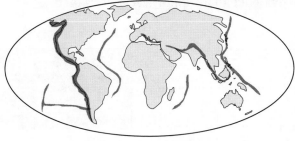

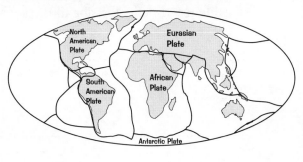

= main earthquake zones

Compare this map to the one showing the tectonic plates.
What do you notice about the main earthquake zones?

....

....

Plate Tectonics

Q1 Wegener studied astronomy at Berlin University in 1904. His fascination with observing identical fossils on both sides of the Atlantic led him to produce his theory of **continental drift** in 1914.

Tick the boxes to say whether the following statements are **true** or **false**.

		True	False
a)	Wegener found that each continent had its own unrelated collection of plant and animal fossils.	☐	☐
b)	The Earth's continents seem to fit together like a big jigsaw.	☐	☐
c)	Rock formations are made of layers, which are different on every continent.	☐	☐
d)	The discovery that the sea floor is spreading suggested that the continents are moving apart. This supports Wegener's theory.	☐	☐
e)	Wegener's theory is now widely accepted because it has been discussed and tested by a range of scientists.	☐	☐
f)	Wegener's theory was **not** readily accepted by scientists at the time.	☐	☐

Q2 Use the words below to complete the passage about Wegener's theory of continental drift.

thousand   countries   tectonics   million   Alfred   continents   movement   Pangaea

Wegener suggested that 300 .... years ago there was one supercontinent,

called .... This supercontinent broke up into smaller chunks — our modern

day .... These chunks are still moving apart. He called his idea the theory

of continental drift. It is the basis of the modern theory of plate ....

Q3 Wegener's theory is now accepted by scientists because it explains lots of different pieces of **evidence**. Briefly describe three pieces of evidence that support Wegener's theory.

1. ....

....

....

2. ....

....

3. ....

....

Volcanic Eruptions

Q1   Number these processes in the correct order to explain **how volcanoes may form**.

☐ Magma rises up through the dense crust to the surface, forming a volcano.

☐ The denser oceanic crust is forced underground (subduction).

☐ Continental crust and oceanic crust collide.

☐ Rock melts underground, forming magma.

Q2   Imagine you live near an active volcano. This volcano only produces **iron-rich basalt** magma.

a)   Describe the type of lava produced from iron-rich basalt magma.

....

b)   Why would it be much more dangerous living near a volcano that produces **silica-rich rhyolite**?

....

Q3   Geologists study volcanoes to try to predict how likely they are to **erupt** in the future.

a)   Describe one sign that might suggest that a volcano is going to erupt.

....

....

b)   Which of the following statements about volcanic eruptions is true? Circle the correct answer.

> **A —** Thanks to past studies, geologists can now say for certain exactly when a volcano will erupt.

> **B —** Geologists cannot say for certain that a volcano is about to erupt, but can often tell if an eruption is likely to happen.

> **C —** Geologists can now predict how likely a volcano is to erupt, but not as accurately as they used to be able to.

___

Top Tips: There are no end of problems with predicting volcanic eruptions. There are likely to be loads of people living near a volcano — it'd be impossible to evacuate them all every time scientists thought there might possibly be an eruption some time soon. It just wouldn't work.

The Three Different Types of Rock

Q1   There are three **main types** of rock.

a) Join up each **rock type** with the correct **method of formation**.

ROCK TYPE   METHOD OF FORMATION

igneous rocks   formed from layers of sediment

sedimentary rocks   formed when magma cools

metamorphic rocks   formed under intense heat and pressure

b) Give an example of:

i) an igneous rock ....

ii) a sedimentary rock ....

iii) a metamorphic rock ....

Q2   Erica notices that the stonework of her local church contains tiny fragments of **sea shells**.

a) Suggest an explanation for this.

....

....

b) Describe how sedimentary rock is 'cemented' together.

....

....

c) Powdered limestone and powdered marble react with other chemicals, such as hydrochloric acid, in an identical fashion. Explain this.

....

....

Top Tips: You might think that rocks are just boring lumps of.... rock. But you'd be wrong — rocks are actually boring lumps of different kinds of rock. And the kind of rock they are depends on how they're formed — and this is the stuff you need to make sure you know.

The Three Different Types of Rock

Q3 Use the words below to complete the paragraph.

heat   metamorphic   igneous   crystals   texture   magma   sedimentary

.... rock forms from layers of sediment compacted at the bottom of seas

over millions of years. As layers build up, the older rock is subjected to ....

and pressure. This can change the .... and mineral structure of the rock

and is how .... rocks form. If the rock gets too hot it melts and is then

known as .... This can force its way to the surface and cool to become

.... rock. These rocks contain minerals in the form of ....

Q4 Below are the processes involved in the formation of **marble**.

a) Number the boxes to show the order in which they occur.

☐ Heat and pressure causes limestone to change into marble.

☐ Dead sea creatures become buried in sediment.

☐ Sea creatures die.

☐ Natural mineral cement sticks the sediment together and limestone forms.

☐ Several layers of sediment build up and compress the lower layers.

b) Describe the differences between limestone and marble.

....

....

c) Marble is a **metamorphic** rock, and granite is an **igneous** rock. Which is harder?

....

Q5 Calcium carbonate can undergo **thermal decomposition**.

a) Explain what thermal decomposition means.

....

....

b) Write out the word and symbol equations for the thermal decomposition of calcium carbonate.

Word equation: ....

Symbol equation: ....

Construction Materials

Q1   Match each **construction material** to the **raw materials** that are needed to make it.

CONSTRUCTION MATERIALS   RAW MATERIALS

cement   ores

bricks   limestone

iron   sand

aluminium   clay

concrete   gravel

Some construction materials are made from more than one raw material from the list.

Q2   Choose from the words below to complete the paragraphs.

clay	sodium carbonate	cement	calcium carbonate	silicon dioxide
melting	extracting	aluminium	fired	bricks	soda

a)   Glass is made by .... limestone (...),

sand (...) and soda (...),

then cooling the mixture.

b)   When moist, ... is a mouldable material made from decomposed rock.

If it is .... at high temperature it can be made into ....

c)   Powdered limestone can also be mixed with ...., then roasted in a

kiln to make ....

Q3   Reinforced concrete is called a '**composite material**'.

a)   Explain why this is. ....

b)   Explain why reinforced concrete is a better construction material than normal concrete.

    ....

Q4   Quarrying limestone can cause a variety of **problems**.

Describe three environmental problems caused by quarrying.

    1. ....

    2. ....

    3. ....

Extracting Pure Copper

Q1 Copper is found in the ground in **ores** such as **chalcopyrite**.

a) How might copper be **extracted** from its ore? ....

b) What is used as the **anode** during the purification of copper by electrolysis?

....

c) Explain how copper is transferred from the anode to the cathode during electrolysis.

....

....

....

Q2 The diagram below shows the purification of copper by electrolysis.

Write the labels that should go at points A–E:

A ....

B ....

C ....

D ....

E ....

Q3 When copper is purified by electrolysis, a **reduction reaction** takes place at the **cathode**, and an **oxidation reaction** happens at the **anode**.

a) Write half-equations for the purification of copper by electrolysis.

i) Cathode: ....

ii) Anode: ....

b) Complete the definition of **reduction** by circling the correct word from each pair:

A reduction reaction is one where a substance **gains / loses** electrons or **gains / loses** oxygen.

Q4 Tick the boxes to show which of the following are good reasons for **recycling copper**.

☐ It's cheaper than mining new copper.   ☐ It uses less energy and therefore less fossil fuel.

☐ You obtain a higher quality of copper.   ☐ It doesn't take much effort.

Module C2 — Chemical Resources

Alloys

Q1 Choose from the words below to complete the paragraph.

sulfur	carbon	bronze	non-metal	alloy	brass	gas

If you mix a metal with another element the resulting mixture is called an

.... The other element may be a ....

An example of this is steel where iron is mixed with small amounts of

.... Alternatively, the other element could be another metal.

An example of this is .... where copper is combined with zinc.

Q2 Metals are mixed with other elements to give them different properties for different uses.

a) Tick the correct boxes to show whether each statement is **true** or **false**.

                                                          True False

    i) Bronze is made of copper and tin. ☐ ☐

    ii) Steel contains copper. ☐ ☐

    iii) Nitinol is made of silver and nickel. ☐ ☐

    iv) Amalgam contains mercury. ☐ ☐

    v) Brass contains zinc. ☐ ☐

    vi) Solder contains aluminium. ☐ ☐

    vii) Brass contains carbon. ☐ ☐

b) Draw lines to join up the following alloys with their uses.

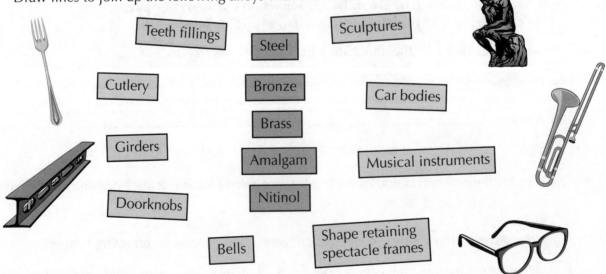

Teeth fillings   Sculptures   Steel

Cutlery   Bronze   Car bodies

Brass

Girders   Amalgam   Musical instruments

Doorknobs   Nitinol

Bells   Shape retaining spectacle frames

Alloys

Q3   The table below shows three types of **bronze** alloy. These alloys only contain tin and copper.

a)   Circle the correct words in each pair to complete the passage below.

> Bronze is much **softer** / **harder** and **stronger** / **weaker** than tin.
> It's also **more** / **less** resistant to corrosion than either copper or tin.

b)   What is the % of copper in **commercial bronze**?

....

c)   What type of bronze do you think is most likely to be used for gold decorations?

....

Alloy	% tin	% copper	Appearance
Hi-Tin Bronze	20	80	Silver
Commercial bronze	10		Dark orange
Hi-copper bronze	5	95	Gold

Q4   Different alloys have different **advantages** and **disadvantages**.

a)   Give one disadvantage of **quick-solidifying solder**.

....

b)   If you could make car bodies from **nitinol**, what advantage would this have?

....

....

....

> Think about how easy it would be to repair after a minor crash.

c)   Suggest a physical property that would make a **brass** screw better than a copper screw.

....

d)   Why are you much more likely to see an outdoor sculpture made of **bronze** than of copper or tin?

....

e)   What property of steel makes it more suitable than iron for:

i) drill bits. ....

ii) ships. ....

Top Tips: The properties of an alloy determine what it's used for, e.g. if you want an alloy that's strong, but lightweight and will harden over time, then a great solution is duralumin (which is aluminium with 4% copper, 1% manganese and some magnesium).

Building Cars

Q1 Use the words below to complete the paragraph.

| salty | iron | reduction | oxidation | iron(II) oxide | iron(III) oxide | rusting | water |

.... is the corrosion of .... If unprotected iron comes into contact with oxygen and ...., a chemical reaction happens. Oxygen reacts with iron to produce hydrated ...., also known as rust. This is known as an .... reaction. This reaction is speeded up if the water is acidic or ....

Q2 In the table below list an advantage and a disadvantage of using **aluminium** and **steel** to make car bodies.

	Steel	**Aluminium**
Advantage		
Disadvantage		

Q3 Fill in the missing labels on the diagram using the words and phrases below. You don't have to use all the words and phrases.

Materials:
Plastic
Copper
Glass
Iron
Natural and synthetic fibres

Advantages:
Light and hard wearing
Strong, easily welded
Electrical conductor
Transparent

Dashboard
Material:
Advantage:

Windows
Material:
Advantage:

Seats
Material:
Advantage:

Electrical wiring
Material:
Advantage:

Q4 Which of the following statements are **true** and which are **false**?

True False

a) Cars are recycled to save natural resources and to reduce landfill use. ☐ ☐

b) There are no laws stating how much of a new car must be recyclable. ☐ ☐

c) It's easy to separate out the non-metal bits of a car. ☐ ☐

d) Currently, scrap metal is the main component of cars that is recycled. ☐ ☐

Module C2 — Chemical Resources

Acids and Bases

Q1   Define the following terms.

a)   Acid ....

b)   Base ....

c)   Alkali ....

Q2   Draw lines to match the substances below to their **universal indicator colour**, **pH** value and **acid/base strength**.

SUBSTANCE	UNIVERSAL INDICATOR COLOUR	PH	ACID/BASE STRENGTH
a) distilled water	purple	5/6	strong alkali
b) rainwater	yellow	8/9	weak alkali
c) caustic soda	dark green/blue	14	weak acid
d) washing-up liquid	red	7	neutral
e) car battery acid	pale green	1	strong acid

Q3 a)   Which is the correct word equation for a **neutralisation reaction**? Circle your answer.

salt + acid → base + water   acid + base → salt + water   acid + water → base + salt

b)   Which of the ions, **H⁺** or **OH⁻**, is found in the largest quantity in:

i) acidic solutions?   ....

ii) alkaline solutions?   ....

iii) a solution with a pH of 10?   ....

iv) lemon juice?   ....

c)   Write out the equation for neutralisation in terms H⁺ and OH⁻ ions.

....

Q4   **Indigestion** is caused by too much acid in the stomach.
Antacid tablets contain bases which neutralise the excess acid.

Joey wanted to test whether some antacid tablets really did **neutralise acid**. He added a tablet to some hydrochloric acid, stirred it until it dissolved and tested the pH of the solution. Further tests were carried out after dissolving a second, third and fourth tablet. His results are shown in the table.

Number of Tablets	pH
0	1
1	2
2	3
3	7
4	9

a)   Describe how the pH changes when antacid tablets are added to the acid.

....

b)   How many tablets were needed to neutralise the acid? ....

Module C2 — Chemical Resources

Reactions of Acids

Q1 Fill in the blanks to complete the word equations for **acids** reacting with **metal oxides** and **metal hydroxides**.

a) hydrochloric acid + lead oxide → .... chloride + water

b) nitric acid + copper hydroxide → copper .... + water

c) sulfuric acid + zinc oxide → zinc sulfate + ...

d) hydrochloric acid + ... oxide → nickel .... + ...

e) .... acid + copper oxide → .... nitrate + ...

f) phosphoric acid + ... hydroxide → sodium .... + ...

Q2 a) Put a tick in the box next to any of the sentences below that are **true**.

i) Alkalis are bases which can't dissolve in water. ☐

ii) Acids react with metal oxides to form a salt and water. ☐

iii) Hydrogen gas is formed when an acid reacts with an alkali. ☐

iv) Salts and water are formed when acids react with metal hydroxides. ☐

v) Sodium hydroxide is an acid that dissolves in water. ☐

b) Use the formulas below to write **symbol equations** for two acid / base reactions.

H_2SO_4 H_2O CuO HCl

H_2O $NaCl$ $CuSO_4$ $NaOH$

1. ....

2. ....

Q3 **Ammonia** can be neutralised by **nitric acid** to form **ammonium nitrate**.

a) Circle the correct formula for ammonia below.

NH_4NO_3 NH_4Cl NH_3 NH_2 NH_4

b) Write down the symbol equation for the reaction between ammonia and nitric acid.

....

c) How is this neutralisation reaction different from most neutralisation reactions?

....

d) Why is ammonium nitrate a particularly good fertiliser?

....

Reactions of Acids

Q4 a) Complete the following equations.

    i) $H_2SO_4 + $ .... $\rightarrow K_2SO_4 + 2H_2O$

    ii) $2HNO_3 + CuO \rightarrow Cu(NO_3)_2 + $ ....

    iii) .... $+ KOH \rightarrow KCl + H_2O$

    iv) $2HCl + $ .... $\rightarrow CuCl_2 + H_2O$

    v) $H_2SO_4 + 2NaOH \rightarrow$ .... $+$ ....

b) **Balance** the following acid/base reactions.

> **i)** $NaOH + H_2SO_4 \rightarrow Na_2SO_4 + H_2O$

> **ii)** $NH_3 + H_2SO_4 \rightarrow (NH_4)_2SO_4$

Q5 **Acids** react with **metal carbonates** in neutralisation reactions.

a) Complete these word equations for the reactions of metal carbonates with acids:

    i) phosphoric acid + ... carbonate $\rightarrow$

        copper .... + water + ...

    ii) .... acid + magnesium .... $\rightarrow$

        .... nitrate + ... + carbon dioxide

    iii) sulfuric acid + lithium carbonate $\rightarrow$ .... + ...+ ....

b) Complete and balance these symbol equations for the reactions of metal carbonates with acids:

    i) .... $HCl + CaCO_3 \rightarrow CaCl_2 + $ .... $+ CO_2$

    ii) $H_2SO_4 + $ .... $\rightarrow Na_2SO_4 + $ .... $+ $ ....

    iii) .... $+ $ .... $\rightarrow Ca(NO_3)_2 + H_2O + CO_2$

    iv) .... $+ Na_2CO_3 \rightarrow$ .... $NaCl + $ .... $+ $ ....

Top Tips: Well take my socks off and paint me blue — that's a lot of equations.
But don't forget, atoms can't be made or lost during a chemical reaction and if you can remember the
different products of neutralisation reactions you can work 'em all out. The clues are all there...

Fertilisers

Q1 Choose from the words to fill in the blanks below.

non-essential	sodium	proteins	growth
phosphorus	carbohydrates	previous	essential

Fertilisers are used to increase crop yield. They provide plants with .... elements needed for ...., making crops grow faster and bigger. These elements include nitrogen, ... and potassium. Fertilisers replace elements in the soil that a .... crop could have used up.

Q2 The graph shows the amount of a **fertiliser** put onto farmland between 1940 and 2000 in one area.

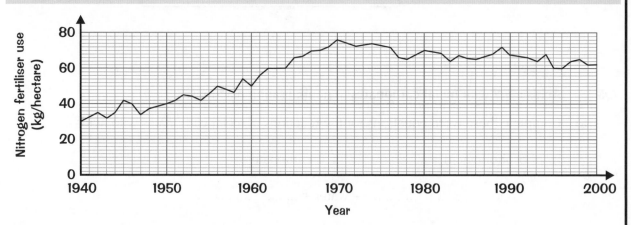

a) What was the first year that **60 kg/hectare or more** of nitrogen fertiliser was used? ....

b) How much nitrogen fertiliser was used in **1970**? ....

c) What is the overall trend in nitrogen fertiliser use **since 1970**?

....

Q3 Number the following stages 1– 6 to describe the process of **eutrophication**.

☐ There is a rapid growth of algae, called an 'algal bloom'.

☐ Sunlight to other plants is blocked, causing them to die.

☐ The amounts of nitrates and phosphates in the water increase.

☐ Fish and other living organisms start to die.

☐ Excess fertiliser runs off fields into rivers and streams.

☐ Aerobic bacteria feed off the dead plants, using up all the oxygen in the water.

Module C2 — Chemical Resources

Fertilisers

Q4 Sophie is concerned about the amount of **fertiliser** that gets washed into **rivers**.

Sophie suggests trapping the fertiliser compounds in **insoluble** pellets to be put on the soil.
Explain why this idea will **not** help to provide the crops with fertiliser.

....

....

Q5 Suggest **three** pieces of advice on the use of fertilisers that could be given to farmers to help prevent **eutrophication**.

1. ....

2. ....

3. ....

Q6 **Ammonium nitrate** is often used as a fertiliser.

a) Name the acid and the base used to make ammonium nitrate.

acid: ....

base: ....

b) Name the element that ammonium nitrate is particularly good at providing to plants.

....

c) Explain why this element is important for plant growth.

....

Q7 Excessive use of fertilisers can cause pollution and eutrophication, but they are still widely used.

a) Given that the population of the world is increasing, explain why fertilisers are so widely used.

....

....

....

b) Ammonia is an important reactant in the production of fertilisers.
What effect do you think the rising population will have on the demand for ammonia?

....

....

Top Tips: Fertilisers are always given a lot of bad press but without them there'd be a lot less food to go round. The trick is not to use too much fertiliser — that'll stop those pesky environmental problems.

Module C2 — Chemical Resources

Preparing Fertilisers

Q1 Tamsin prepares **ammonium sulfate** in the lab using the apparatus shown in the diagram.

a) Name the two reactants Tamsin needs to use to make ammonium sulfate.

1. ....

2. ....

b) Suggest what piece of apparatus Tamsin used to accurately measure 25.0 cm³ of solution B.

....

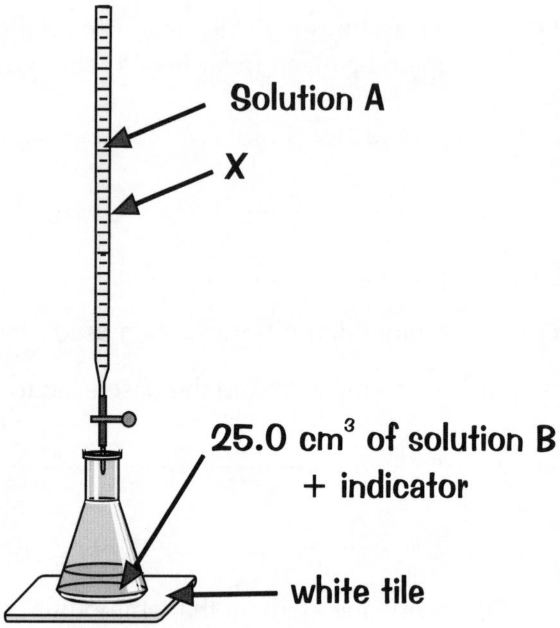

c) Name the piece of apparatus shown in the diagram that's labelled **X**.

....

d) What type of reaction is occurring?

....

e) Name an indicator Tamsin could use to decide when the reaction is finished.

....

Solution A

X

25.0 cm³ of solution B + indicator

white tile

f) Describe the method used to find the end point of the reaction

....

....

....

Tamsin finds that she needs 12.6 cm³ of solution A for the reaction.
She repeats the experiment to obtain **pure** crystals of ammonium sulfate.

g) What important **difference** must she make to her experimental procedure to produce **pure** ammonium sulfate?

....

h) What volume of solution A must she add? ....

i) How can Tamsin get ammonium sulfate crystals from her ammonium sulfate solution?

....

....

The Haber Process

Q1   The Haber process is used to make **ammonia**.

a)   Write a balanced symbol equation for the reaction that takes place in the Haber process.

.... + ... ⇌ ....

b)   Explain what the symbol ⇌ tells you about this reaction.

....

Q2   The **industrial conditions** for the Haber process are carefully chosen.

a)   What conditions are used? Tick one box.

☐ 1000 atmospheres, 450 °C	☐ 200 atmospheres, 1000 °C	☐ 450 atmospheres, 200 °C	☐ 200 atmospheres, 450 °C

b)   Explain why the pressure used is chosen.

....

....

Q3   In the Haber process, the reaction is affected by the temperature.

a)   What effect will raising the temperature have on the **amount** of ammonia formed?

....

b)   Explain why a high temperature is still used industrially.

....

c)   What happens to the leftover nitrogen and hydrogen? ....

Q4   The Haber process uses an **iron catalyst**.

a)   What effect does this have on the % yield? ....

b)   Iron catalysts are cheap. What effect does using one have on the **cost** of producing the ammonia? Explain your answer.

....

....

Top Tips: Changing the conditions in a reversible reaction to get more product sounds great, but don't forget that those conditions might make the reaction too slow to be profitable.

Minimising the Cost of Production

Q1 Use the following words to complete the blanks.

| yield | sufficient | optimum | rate | recycled | lowest |

.... conditions are chosen to give the .... production cost per kg of product. This may mean that the conditions used do not have the highest .... of reaction or the highest percentage .... of product. However, both the rate and the yield must be high enough to give a .... daily yield of product. A low percentage yield is acceptable if the starting materials can be .... and reacted again.

Q2 Explain how the following affect the **production costs** of making a new substance.

a) Catalysts ....

....

b) Recycling raw materials ....

....

c) Automation ....

....

d) High temperatures ....

....

e) Very high pressure ....

....

Q3 A pharmaceutical company tests two production processes for producing a new drug. Rupert records both the total **production cost** and the total **yield** for each process over a one-week period.

a) Calculate the cost per g of drug for each process.

....

....

....

....

b) Suggest why the company decides to use process B, even though it has a higher production cost.

....

Salt

Q1 Indicate whether the following statements about obtaining salt are **true** or **false**.

True False

a) In the UK most salt is obtained by evaporation in flat open tanks. ☐ ☐

b) There are massive deposits of rock salt in Cheshire. ☐ ☐

c) Salt can be mined by pumping hot water underground. ☐ ☐

d) Some holes left by mining salt must be filled in, or they could cause subsidence. ☐ ☐

Q2 **Circle** the correct answer for each of the questions below.

a) One of the products of the electrolysis of brine is chlorine. You can test for it by:

Using a glowing splint — chlorine will relight it.

Using damp litmus paper — chlorine will bleach it.

Using universal indicator — chlorine will turn it purple.

b) Two of the products of electrolysis are reacted together to make household bleach. They are:

Chlorine and hydrogen.

Chlorine and sodium hydroxide.

Hydrogen and sodium hydroxide.

Q3 The diagram shows the **industrial set-up** used to electrolyse concentrated brine.

a) Identify the substances labelled A, B, C and D on the diagram. Choose from the options in the box below.

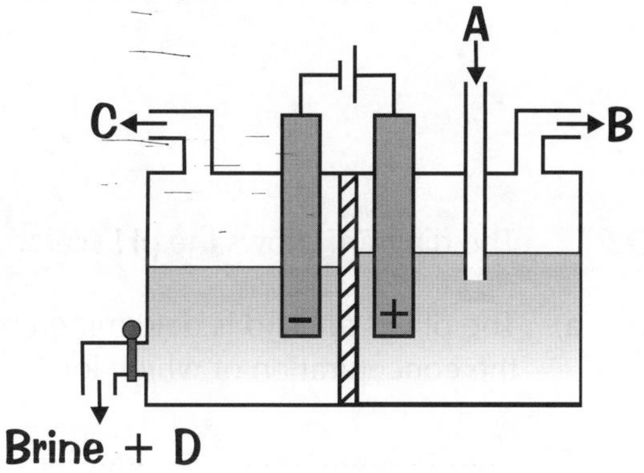

Na	O_2	Cl_2	H_2
brine	NaOH	H_2O	

A .... B ....

C .... D ....

b) Write **balanced** half-equations for the reactions that occur during the electrolysis of this salt solution.

Make sure the charges balance.

Anode: ....

Cathode: ....

c) **i)** State the electrode where oxidation take place. ....

ii) State the electrode where reduction take place. ....

d) Why are inert electrodes used?

....

Module C2 — Chemical Resources

Mixed Questions — Module C2

Q1   **Limestone** is a sedimentary rock.

a)   Describe the main steps in the formation of sedimentary rocks.

....

....

....

b)   Complete the following equation to show the **thermal decomposition** of limestone.

$CaCO_3 \rightarrow$ .... + ...

c)   Limestone can be processed to form useful building materials. Complete the flow diagram.

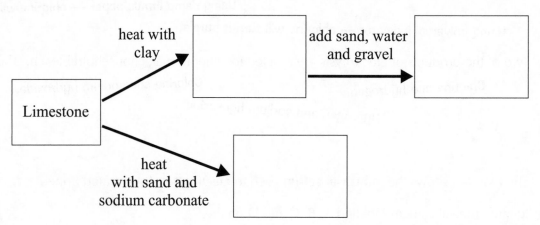

Q2   The diagram shows the **pH scale**.

a)   The pH of an acid is determined by the concentration of which ion?

....

| 1 | 2 | 3 | 4 | 5 | 6 | 7 | 8 | 9 | 10 | 11 | 12 | 13 |

black coffee   magnesium hydroxide

b)   The pH values of black coffee and magnesium hydroxide are marked on the diagram.

i)   Is black coffee neutral, acidic or alkaline?   ....

ii)   Is magnesium hydroxide neutral, acidic or alkaline? ....

c)   Does universal indicator show a **sudden** or **gradual** change in colour as pH changes?

....

d)   Indigestion is caused by excess acid in the stomach. Magnesium hydroxide, $Mg(OH)_2$, is used in indigestion remedies. Explain how magnesium hydroxide can help with indigestion.

....

Mixed Questions — Module C2

Q3   Copper is a metal with a variety of uses.

a)   Copper is dug out of the ground as an **ore**. Explain what an **ore** is.

....

b)   Copper is used in **alloys**. Circle the alloys below which contain copper.

　　　bronze　　amalgam　　brass　　steel　　solder　　nitinol

c)   The diagram below shows how copper is purified. Label the **anode** and the **cathode**.

d)   What makes copper atoms go into solution as ions?

....

....

e)   Which electrode increases in size during the electrolysis?

....

f)   What is purified copper used for in cars? Why is this?

....

g)   Name another **metal** which is used in cars. What part of the car is it used for and why?

....

....

h)   Suggest two pros of **recycling** the copper and other metals used in cars.

....

....

Q4   A **subduction zone** occurs where an oceanic plate and a continental plate collide.

a)   What happens to the plates at a subduction zone?

....

....

b)   Explain how volcanoes are formed near to a subduction zone.

....

....

c)   Is the type of rock formed from volcanoes metamorphic, sedimentary or igneous?

....

Mixed Questions — Module C2

Q5 Chlorine, hydrogen and sodium hydroxide are produced by **electrolysing brine**.

a) Place each of the uses listed below into the correct box to show whether it is a use of chlorine, hydrogen or sodium hydroxide. Some uses may belong in more than one box.

PVC   soap   solvents   margarine   disinfecting water   bleach   ammonia

CHLORINE	HYDROGEN	SODIUM HYDROXIDE

b) Chlorine and sodium hydroxide are made by the **chlor-alkali industry**.
Apart from making useful products, give a reason why the chlor-alkali industry is so important.

....

c) Give the four ions that are present in brine.

1 .... 2 .... 3 .... 4 ....

d) i) What is produced at the anode during the electrolysis of brine? ....

ii) What is produced at the cathode during the electrolysis of brine? ....

Q6 The **Haber process** is used to produce ammonia.

a) Give **four factors** on which the cost of producing ammonia depends.

....

....

b) The temperature and pressure conditions for the Haber process could be described as
'**a compromise**'. With reference to these conditions explain what the 'compromise' is.

....

....

....

c) Ammonia is used to produce ammonium nitrate fertiliser.
Explain how excess fertiliser on fields can kill fish in local rivers.

....

....

....

Using the Sun's Energy

Q1   Choose from the words below to complete the passage about how **photocells** generate electricity. Each word may be used once, more than once, or not at all.

semiconductor	metal	atoms	efficient	neutrons	DC	protons	AC	electrons	silicon	track

Many photocells are made of ...., which is a ....

When sunlight falls on the cell, silicon .... absorb some of the energy of the

light, which knocks some of their .... loose. These ....

then flow around a circuit to give a .... current. Photocells are most

.... if they're made to .... the Sun's movement.

Q2   The diagram shows a photocell generating direct current (DC).

sunlight   photocell   bulb   electric current (DC)

a)   What is meant by **direct** current?

....

b)   Explain how **sunlight intensity**, **surface area** and **distance from the light source** of a photocell affect its electrical power output.

....

....

....

Q3   Photocells can also be called **solar cells**.

a)   Give two advantages of using solar cells to generate electricity.

1. ....

2. ....

b)   Give one disadvantage of using solar cells to generate electricity.

....

Top Tips: The Sun produces a huge amount of energy and will continue to do so for millions of years to come. Handy. Use your own energy more efficiently in your exams — revise, practise and when you're in the exam **read** the questions carefully. Seems obvious — but it's easy to write what you want to write and not what the examiner wants to read. Then you lose marks. What a waste.

Solar and Wind Power

Q1   **Wind turbines** can be used to generate electricity from **moving air**.

What is the original source of the wind energy that turns the turbine?

What causes the air to move?

turbine blades

electrical output

generator

....

Q2   Tick the boxes to show whether these statements are **true** or **false**.

True   False

a)   Gravity from the Moon causes wind.   ☐ ☐

b)   Passive solar heating can only work where it's constantly sunny.   ☐ ☐

c)   All infrared radiation passes easily through glass.   ☐ ☐

d)   Wind turbines can only be sited on hilltops.   ☐ ☐

Q3   **Passive solar heating** can be used to heat a building directly. Circle the correct word in each of the following sentences.

a)   Glass **lets through** / **absorbs** radiation from the Sun.

b)   Objects get **cooler** / **warmer** when they absorb radiation.

c)   **Black** / **white** objects absorb the most radiation.

d)   Warm objects emit **infrared** / **ultraviolet** radiation which has a **shorter** / **longer** wavelength than radiation from the Sun.

e)   Glass **lets through** / **reflects** the radiation emitted by warm objects.

Q4   People often **object** to **wind turbines** being put up near to where they live.

a)   Give two reasons why they might **object**.

....

....

....

b)   List three arguments in favour of using wind turbines to generate electricity.

1. ....

2. ....

3. ....

Producing and Distributing Electricity

Q1 Complete the passage by choosing from the words given.

National	Express	Grid	power stations	worms	farms	consumers	generated

Most electricity is produced by .... The ....

.... is the network of pylons and cables which covers the whole

country. It enables electricity .... almost anywhere to be supplied

to .... almost anywhere, e.g. homes and ....

Q2 In a large **power station**, there are several steps involved in making electricity. Number these steps in the right order — from 1 to 5.

☐ Hot steam rushes through a turbine and makes it spin.

☐ Electricity is produced by the spinning generator.

☐ A fossil fuel such as coal is burned to release heat.

☐ The spinning turbine makes the generator spin too.

☐ Water is heated in the boiler and turned to steam.

Q3 The city of Fakeville decides to replace its old coal-fired power station. They have to choose between using gas or nuclear power.

Give one **disadvantage** of each choice:

a) **Gas** ....

....

b) **Nuclear power** ....

....

Q4 Both wood and coal produce **carbon dioxide** when they are burned.

a) Wood from fast-growing trees is a **renewable** resource. Explain what this means.

....

b) Explain why burning wood is 'carbon neutral' but burning coal is not.

....

....

....

The Dynamo Effect

Q1 A simple **dynamo** can be made by rotating a magnet end to end inside a coil of wire.

a) What happens to the magnetic field when the magnet turns half a turn?

....

b) What is created in the wire by this rotation?

....

Q2 Moving a **magnet** inside a **coil** of **copper wire** produces a trace on a cathode ray oscilloscope.

Coil

Bar magnet

Cathode ray oscilloscope

Traces on oscilloscope

A   B

C   D

When the magnet was pushed inside the coil, Trace A was produced on the screen.

a) Explain how Trace B could be produced.

....

b) Explain how Trace C could be produced.

....

c) Explain how Trace D could be produced.

....

Q3 Look at the simple **AC generators** sketched below.

Coil spread over greater area

Quicker rotation

Stronger magnet

A ☐   B ☐   C ☐

One of the generators labelled A - C will **not** induce a higher voltage than the generator in the box. Tick the box next to the generator.

Module P2 — Living for the Future

Supplying Electricity Efficiently

Q1 Number these statements 1 to 5 to show the order of the steps that are needed to deliver energy to Mrs Miggins' house so that she can boil the kettle.

	An electrical current flows through power cables across the country.
	Mrs Miggins boils the kettle for tea.
	Electrical energy is generated in power stations.
	The voltage of the supply is raised.
	The voltage of the supply is reduced.

Q2 Each of the following sentences is incorrect. Write out a correct version of each.

a) The National Grid transmits energy at high voltage and high current.

....

b) A step-up transformer is used to reduce the voltage of the supply before electricity is transmitted.

....

c) Using a high current makes sure there is not much energy wasted.

....

Q3 Use the **efficiency formula** to complete the table.

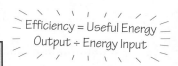
Efficiency = Useful Energy Output ÷ Energy Input

Total Energy Input (J)	Useful Energy Output (J)	Efficiency
2000	1500	
	2000	0.50
4000		0.25

Q4 One litre of oil produces 6 MJ of energy when it is completely burned in air.
A power station with an overall efficiency of 30% consumes oil at the rate of 40 litres per second.
Calculate the **total energy loss per second** for the power station.

....

....

Power

Q1 The **current** an appliance draws depends on its **power** rating. Complete the table below, showing the power rating and current drawn by various appliances at mains voltage — **230 V**.

Appliance	Power (W)	Current (A)
Kettle	2600	
Radio	13	
Laptop computer		3.2
Lamp		0.17

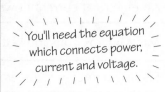

You'll need the equation which connects power, current and voltage.

Q2 Boris puts his **2 kW** electric heater on for 3 hours.

a) Calculate how many **kilowatt-hours** of electrical energy the heater uses.

.... kWh.

b) Boris gets his electricity supply from Ivasparkco. They charge 7p per kilowatt-hour. Work out the **cost** of the energy calculated in part (a).

....

....

c) Boris's wife grumbles at him for leaving a 60 W lamp on overnight — about 9 hours every night. Boris says his wife uses **more energy** by using an 8 kW shower for 15 minutes every day.

Is Boris right? Calculate how much energy each person uses and compare your results.

....

....

....

Q3 Mr Havel recently received his **electricity bill**. Unfortunately, he tore off the bottom part to write a shopping list.

a) How many **Units** of energy did Mr Havel use in the three months from June to September?

....

b) What would the bill have said for 'total cost'?

....

....

Customer : Havel, V

Date   Meter Reading

11 06 06   34259
10 09 06   34783

Total Cost @ 9.7p per Unit

Power

Q4 Off-peak electricity is sometimes cheaper than electricity at peak times.

a) Give an example of an electrical appliance designed to use off-peak electricity.

....

b) i) Give one advantage for the consumer of using off-peak electricity:

....

ii) Give one advantage for the electricity generating company of using off-peak electricity:

....

....

Q5 Pumped storage power stations work by using off-peak electricity to pump water into a holding reservoir at night. In the daytime they release water from the reservoir to generate electricity, which is then sold to the National Grid at peak rate prices. The table below shows data for a typical pumped storage power station.

	Night time (input)	Daytime (output)
Running time	7 hours	5 hours
Power	275 MW	288 MW
Cost per kWh	3.7p	7.2p

Be careful — watch out for units.

a) Calculate the cost of electricity used in the night time operation.

....

....

b) Calculate the value (in £) of the electricity generated in the daytime operation.

....

....

Q6 A tumble drier operating on a 230 V household supply uses a current of 10 A.

a) Calculate the power rating of the tumble drier in kW.

....

b) Peak time electricity costs 11.3p/Unit. Off peak electricity costs 6.0p/Unit. Calculate the **money saved** if a tumble drier is operated for 2 hours during off peak hours rather than at peak time.

....

....

The Greenhouse Effect

Q1 The diagram below shows how the 'greenhouse effect' keeps the Earth warm.
Use the descriptions **A** to **E** to label the diagram. The first one has been done for you.

A
The Earth absorbs
radiation from the Sun.

B
The Earth emits
heat radiation.

C
Greenhouse gases
absorb radiation from Earth.

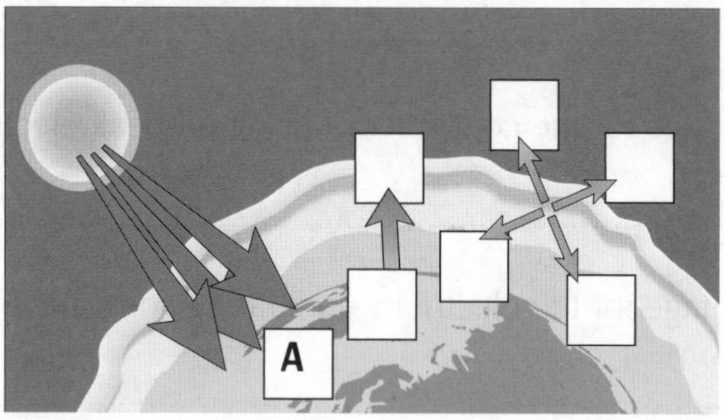

E
The greenhouse gases
emit some heat radiation
into space.

D
The greenhouse
gases emit some heat
towards Earth.

Q2 Tick the boxes next to any **greenhouse gases** below.

nitrogen ☐   water vapour ☐   carbon dioxide ☐

oxygen ☐   methane ☐   helium ☐

Q3 Which of the statements below is the best description
of the **greenhouse effect**? Circle A, B, C or D.

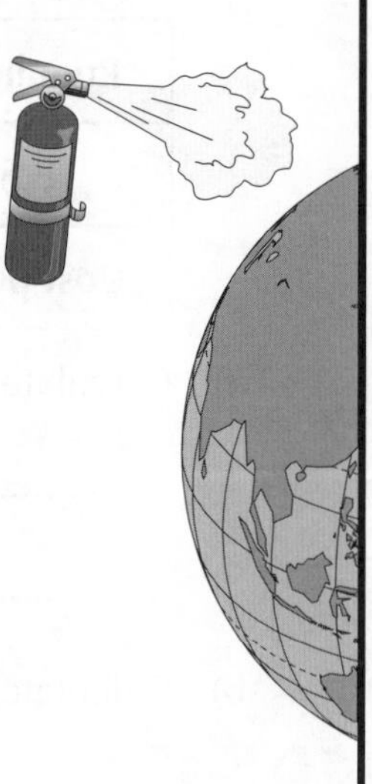

A   Global warming caused by man's impact on the environment.

B   A process which keeps the Earth warmer than it would otherwise be.

C   A chemical reaction in the atmosphere which releases heat energy.

D   The natural heating effect of the Sun.

Q4 Over the last 200 years or so the atmospheric concentration of
some **greenhouse gasses**, like CO_2 and methane, has increased.

a) i) Give one natural source of atmospheric CO_2.

....

ii) Describe two ways in which humans have contributed to the increase in atmospheric CO_2.

....

....

b)   List some natural and man-made sources of methane.

....

....

Global Warming and Climate Change

Q1 Complete the passage by choosing from the words below.

fallen	clouds	carbon	pressures	greenhouse
temperatures	increased	butterfly	sulfur	sea

Global .... have .... in recent years.

This is due to an increased .... effect caused by

'too much' .... dioxide in the atmosphere.

Q2 Below are five statements about climate change.
Tick the boxes to show which statements are **descriptions of data** and which are possible **explanations of data**.

	Description of Data	Explanation of Data
a) Global temperatures are steadily increasing.	☐	☐
b) Carbon dioxide levels in the atmosphere are steadily increasing.	☐	☐
c) The rise in atmospheric carbon dioxide concentration is causing a rise in global temperatures.	☐	☐
d) There are more extreme weather events every year.	☐	☐
e) The Earth's increasingly extreme weather is caused by global warming.	☐	☐

Q3 Scientists use **climate models** to predict how human activity and natural phenomena will affect the Earth's climate in the future.

a) Professor Cloud has developed a new climate model. She tests it by putting in some data about the climate as it was 10 years ago, and getting the model to predict the present day climate.

Explain how this helps Professor Cloud know whether her new climate model is any good.

....

....

....

b) Describe how dust from human activities can affect the climate.

....

....

Top Tips: Climate models are super-useful, but they aren't always perfect. They get better over time as scientists gather more data. With something as serious as global warming though, we can't afford to wait and find out if the climate models are exactly right because then it might be too late.

Nuclear Radiation

Q1 Complete the passage using the words given below. You will not have to use all the words.

ion	negative	less	more	electron	further	less far	positive

When ionising radiation interacts with atoms it sometimes causes the atom to lose an

.... , leaving behind a ....

Radiations which are more ionising travel .... into a material and

tend to cause .... damage in the material they have penetrated.

Q2 Complete the table below by choosing the **correct word** from each column.

Radiation Type	Ionising power weak/moderate/strong	Relative size no mass/small/large	Penetrating power low/moderate/high
Alpha			
Beta			
Gamma			

Q3 Brian was investigating three radioactive sources — A, B and C.
Radiation from each source was directed towards target sheets of **paper**, **aluminium** and an **unknown sheet**. Counters were used to detect where radiation passed through the target sheets.

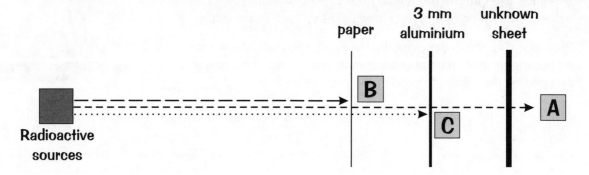

Results:
Source A — emits gamma radiation, which was partially absorbed by the unknown sheet.
Source B — the radiation was stopped by the paper.
Source C — the radiation was stopped by the aluminium.

a) What type of radiation is emitted by:

i) Source B? ....

ii) Source C? ....

b) Suggest what the unknown sheet was made from.

....

Module P2 — Living for the Future

Uses of Nuclear Radiation

Q1 The following sentences explain how a **smoke detector** works, but they are in the wrong order. Put them in order by labelling them 1 (first) to 6 (last).

Assume that a fire starts a while after the smoke detector was installed.

☐ The circuit is broken so no current flows.

1 The radioactive source emits alpha particles.

☐ A current flows between the electrodes — the alarm stays off.

☐ The alarm sounds.

☐ The air between the electrodes is ionised by the alpha particles.

☐ A fire starts and smoke particles absorb the alpha radiation.

Q2 The diagram shows how **beta radiation** can be used in the control of paper thickness in a paper mill.

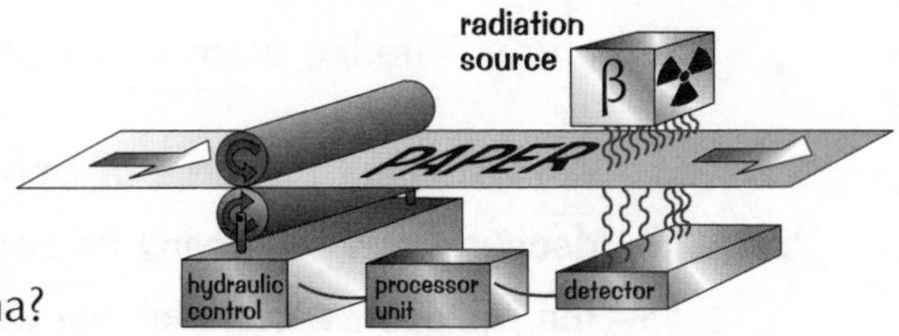

Why is beta radiation used, rather than alpha or gamma?

....

....

Q3 Radiation can be used to **sterilise** surgical instruments.

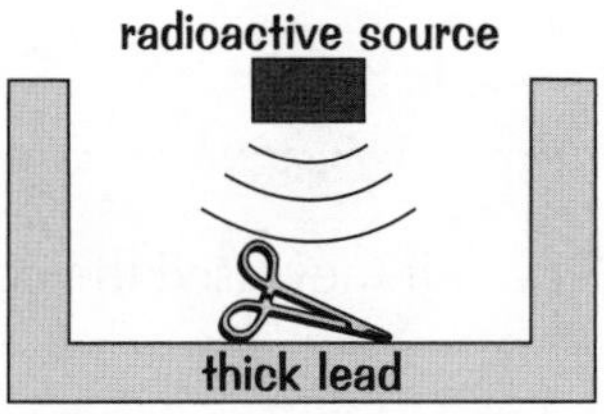

a) What kind of radioactive source is used, and why? In your answer, mention the **type** of radiation emitted (alpha, beta and gamma) and how **quickly** the source decays.

....

....

....

b) What is the purpose of the thick lead?

....

....

Q4 **Gamma radiation** can be used to test turbine blades in jet engines.

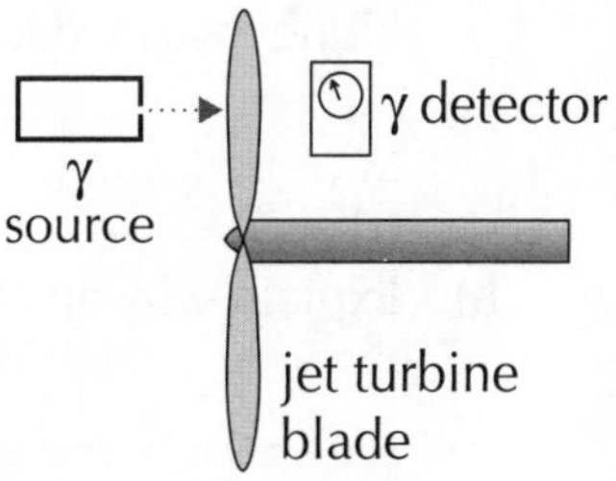

Explain how the test would detect a crack in the turbine blade.

....

....

....

Uses of Nuclear Radiation

Q5 Eviloilco knows that its oil pipeline is **leaking**, somewhere between points A and B.

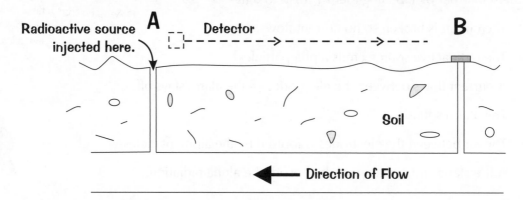

This is how Eviloilco plans to find the leak.

> We will inject a source of alpha radiation into the pipeline at point A. (This source decays slowly — giving us better value for money in the long term.) After injecting the radioactive material, we will pass a sensor along the surface above the pipeline — and so detect where radiation is escaping, hence pinpointing the leak.

a) Give two reasons why Eviloilco has made a bad choice of radioactive source.

....

....

b) Even if they used the correct type of radioactive source, their plan would still fail. Why?

....

Q6 A patient has a **radioactive source** injected into her body to test her kidneys.

A healthy kidney will get rid of the radioactive material quickly (to the bladder). Damaged kidneys take longer to do this.

The results of the test, for both the patient's kidneys, are shown opposite.

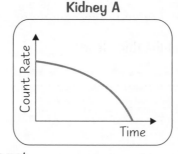

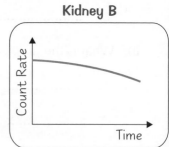

a) Explain how the doctor knew which kidney was working well and which was not.

....

b) Explain why an alpha source would **not** be suitable for this investigation.

....

....

Nuclear Power

Q1 Tick the boxes to show which of these statements are **true** and which are **false**.

True False

a) In a nuclear power station, radon is used to make heat. ☐ ☐

b) The energy released from radioactive material is used to produce steam. ☐ ☐

c) Carbon dioxide is a waste product of nuclear power. ☐ ☐

d) Nuclear reactions release a similar amount of energy to chemical reactions. ☐ ☐

e) Uranium is a renewable energy resource. ☐ ☐

Q2 Outline three **disadvantages** of using nuclear power.

1. ....

2. ....

3. ....

Q3 State one **advantage** of nuclear power over generating electricity from:

a) fossil fuels

....

b) renewable energy

....

Q4 Use the words and phrases below to complete the passage.

Some words may be used more than once.

control rods	fuel	plutonium	nuclear weapons	uranium

Used uranium .... from nuclear power stations can be reprocessed.

Reprocessing produces more .... and some ....

The .... can be reused in the reactor and the ....

can be used to make ....

Top Tips: Nuclear fuel can provide loads more energy than the same mass of fossil fuel. Given the current concerns about CO_2 emissions from burning fossil fuels, you can see why many people see nuclear fuel as an attractive alternative. Nuclear waste is really dangerous though.

Danger from Radioactive Materials

Q1 Two scientists are discussing their samples of radioactive material.

a) One of the scientists is taking sensible safety precautions, but the other is not.
Describe three things which the careless scientist is doing wrong.

1. ....

2. ....

3. ....

b) Describe another way the scientists can reduce their exposure to radiation,
besides using special apparatus or clothing.

....

c) How should radioactive samples be stored when they are not in use?

....

Q2 **High-level** radioactive waste is **harder** to dispose of than low-level waste.

a) For how long can high-level waste stay radioactive?

....

b) High level nuclear waste is disposed of by burying it deep underground.
What is often done to the waste before it's buried?

....

....

c) Scientists have to find suitable sites to bury high-level nuclear waste.
Why must sites for disposal of high-level waste be geologically stable?

....   _Geologically unstable can_
mean prone to earthquakes.

....

....

The Solar System

Q1 This diagram shows the major bodies in the Solar System. It **isn't to scale**.

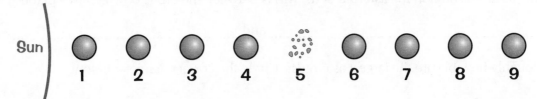

Sun 1 2 3 4 5 6 7 8 9

In the table below, write the correct number under each name to show its position in the Solar System.

Body	Mars	Jupiter	Asteroids	Venus	Saturn	Neptune	Earth	Mercury	Uranus
Number									

Q2 When Robert looks up into the night sky, he sees **stars** and **planets** (as long as it's a clear night).

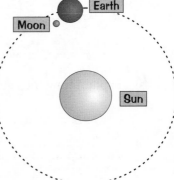

Give three ways in which the planets that Robert sees are different from the stars he sees.

1. ....

2. ....

3. ....

Q3 The **Moon** orbits the **Earth** which is itself orbiting the **Sun** as shown. The diagram is not to scale.

a) What is the name of the type of force that causes circular motion?

....

b) Name the force which keeps the Earth and Moon in their orbits.

....

c) Draw an arrow on the diagram to show the direction of the force acting on the Earth which keeps it orbiting the Sun.

d) Explain why the Moon is not pulled away from the Earth by the Sun.

....

....

....

Asteroids and Comets

Q1   As well as planets, there are **asteroids** orbiting the Sun.

a)   The asteroids orbit in the **asteroid belt**. This is between the orbits of which two planets?

.... and ....

b)   Roughly how big are the largest asteroids? Circle the correct diameter below.

      A 1000 mm   **C 1000 m**

        B 1000 cm   **D 1000 km**

Q2   Choose from the words and phrases in the box below to complete the passage. Words can be used more than once.

meteorites	asteroids	burn up
stars	atmosphere	meteors shooting

.... are rocks or dust that enter the Earth's atmosphere.

As they pass through the .... they ....

and are seen as .... Remains of the

.... that land on the Earth are called ....

Q3   Scientists think that a very large **asteroid** struck the Earth at the Yucatán peninsula in the Gulf of Mexico about 65 million years ago and caused the **extinction** of over half the species on Earth.

a)   What **evidence** is there that asteroids have collided with the Earth?

....

....

b)   Explain how the asteroid's impact might have led to the extinction of so many species.

....

....

....

Top Tips: Don't get asteroids and comets mixed up. Asteroids stay in the asteroid belt where they belong (well, they do most of the time), and comets have really long orbits that take them even further out than the furthest planets, and really close in to the Sun.

Asteroids and Comets

Q4 The diagram shows the orbit of a **comet** around the Sun.

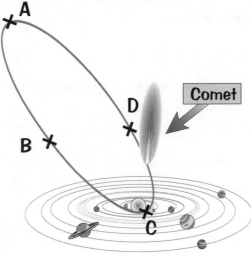

a) What is the name of the **shape** of the comet's orbit?

....

b) Write down the letters that show where the comet's speed is at its:

i) maximum: ....

ii) minimum: ....

c) Explain your answers to part b).

....

....

d) i) What are comets made of?

....

ii) What causes the comet to have a 'tail'?

....

Q5 The asteroids in the asteroid belt haven't **clumped together** to form a single planet, even though each exerts a gravitational pull on the others. Suggest why they **haven't** formed a single planet.

Think about the sizes of the planets — especially the planets nearest to the asteroids.

....

....

....

NEOs and the Moon

Q1 Some astronomers work on finding **Near Earth Objects** (NEOs).

a) What are Near Earth Objects?

....

b) Explain why it is important to track their trajectories.

....

....

c) Why are NEOs difficult to monitor?

....

....

d) Describe one thing that could be done if an NEO was heading for a collision with the Earth.

....

....

Q2 The following diagrams show how scientists think the **Moon** was formed.

1) A small planet collided side-on with the Earth.

2) The iron cores of the planets fused at very high temperatures.

3) Low density bits flew off and orbited the Earth.

4) The bits eventually came together as the Moon.

Explain how the following facts about the Earth and the Moon support this theory.

a) The Moon is less dense than the Earth.

....

....

b) The Moon doesn't have a big iron core, but the Earth does.

....

....

c) The Moon is made of materials with high melting points and boiling points.

....

....

Beyond the Solar System

Q1   One of the following statements is **not true**. Circle the letter next to the false statement.

   A   A galaxy is made up of billions of stars.

   B   The distance between galaxies can be millions of times the distance between stars.

   C   Gravity is the force which keeps stars apart.

   D   Galaxies rotate in space.

   E   Planets are formed from the same clouds of gas and dust as stars.

Q2   The **light year** is used as a unit of length by astronomers.

   a)   Write down a definition of a light year.

   ....

   b)   Calculate the length **in km** of one **light year** given that:

   1 day = 24 hours

   1 year = 365.25 days

   Speed of light = 3×10^8 m/s.

   Watch out for units — the answer has to be in km, not m.

   ....

   ....

   c)   The Milky Way is about 100 000 light years in diameter. The Solar System is about halfway along one of the Galaxy's spiral arms. Use your answer to part b) to calculate how far we are from the centre of the Galaxy, in **km**, giving your answer in standard form, to 3 significant figures.

   ....

   ....

Q3   **Black holes** are the last stages in the lives of big stars.

   a)   Explain in terms of gravitational attraction why black holes are black.

   ....

   ....

   ....

   b)   How do scientists detect black holes?

   ....

   ....

Exploring the Solar System

Q1   Scientists estimate that a round trip to **Mars** would take astronauts up to **2 years** to complete.
Identify four problems associated with such a journey.

1. ....

2. ....

3. ....

4. ....

Q2   Scientists have already landed **unmanned probes** on Mars.

a)   Outline two advantages of using unmanned probes.

....

....

b)   Describe one disadvantage of using unmanned probes.

....

c)   Describe how information collected by the probe could be sent back to Earth.

....

Q3   Not all unmanned probes are designed to land on a body's surface.

a)   What kinds of data can be collected **without** landing on the surface?

....

....

b)   Probes designed to land safely on the surface often carry exploration **rovers**
which can explore their surroundings and collect data.

i)   What kinds of investigation could be carried out by an exploration rover?

....

....

ii)   Several probes intended to land on Mars have failed — they've been too badly
damaged to work. Suggest why it is so difficult to land a probe safely.

....

....

....

The Origin of the Universe

Q1 The Big Bang theory is the accepted scientific explanation for the origin of the Universe.

a) Complete this passage using the words supplied below.

expansion	matter	energy	expand	age	explosion

Many scientists believe that the universe started with all the ....

and .... in one small space. There was a huge ....

and the material started to .... Scientists can estimate the

.... of the universe using the current rate of ....

b) Why are estimates of the age of the Universe quite **unreliable**?

....

Q2 Here are some statements about the expansion of the Universe. Tick the boxes
to show whether each statement describes **data** or is part of an **explanation**.

Data Explanation

a) Most galaxies are moving away from us. ☐ ☐

b) The further away a galaxy is, the faster it is moving away. ☐ ☐

c) The Universe is expanding. ☐ ☐

d) The Universe started from a single point. ☐ ☐

e) Microwave radiation comes from all over the Universe. ☐ ☐

Q3 Many cosmologists believe that the Universe began with a **Big Bang**.

a) Briefly describe the Big Bang theory.

....

....

b) According to the Big Bang theory, what is happening to space itself?

....

Q4 What **evidence** is there to support the idea that the Universe began with a 'Big Bang'?
Include a brief explanation of **red-shift** and **cosmic background radiation** in your answer.

....

....

....

....

....

The Life Cycle of Stars

Q1   A star in its **stable** phase **doesn't get bigger or smaller**, even though there are forces tending to make it expand and forces trying to make it contract.

a) What causes the outward pressure on the star?

....

b) What is the force pulling the star inwards? ....

c) Why doesn't the star expand or contract?

....

d) What is another name for a star in its stable phase? ....

Q2   Stars are formed from clouds of dust and gas.

a) **Why** does the material come together?

....

b) Where does the **heat and light energy** emitted by a star come from?

....

Q3   Old stars eventually turn into **red giants**.

a) What causes a star to become a red giant? ....

....

b) Why is a red giant red? ....

....

Q4   Complete the passage below to describe what eventually happens to red giants.

A small star will eject gas and dust as a ...., leaving

a dense core called a .... A bigger star will

explode as a ...., leaving a very dense core

called a .... The biggest stars

form .... instead.

You might need two words to fill the gap.

Due to printing restrictions, red giants are unavailable.

Q5   Explain what happens in a big star **as it changes** from a red supergiant to a supernova.

....

....

Galileo and Copernicus

Q1   Circle the correct word in the following sentences.

a)   The planets all orbit the Earth in a **geocentric** / **heliocentric** model.

b)   **Galileo** / **Copernicus** introduced a heliocentric model in 1543.

c)   The Copernican model states that the planets all orbit the **Sun** / **Milky Way**.

d)   The orbits of the planets in the Copernican model are all perfect **circles** / **ellipses**.

e)   In the Copernican model the Sun is at the centre of the **Universe** / **Solar System**.

f)   We now know that the planets actually have **circular** / **elliptical** orbits.

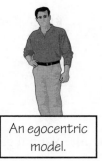

An egocentric model.

Q2   Galileo made some observations of Jupiter that helped to provide evidence for the Copernican model of the solar system.

a)   What technological advance helped Galileo to look at Jupiter?

....

b)   Briefly describe what Galileo saw when making his observations of Jupiter and Venus.

....

....

....

....

c)   Explain how Galileo's observations helped provide evidence for the Copernican model.

....

....

....

d)   Why were Galileo's ideas controversial at the time?

....

....

Top Tips: For as long as humans have looked at the sky they've tried to find an explanation for how it all works — it takes a long time and technological advances for some ideas to change. Make sure you know what Copernicus' great idea was, and what Galileo saw that showed it might be right.

Module P2 — Living for the Future

Mixed Questions — Module P2

Q1   Electricity is generated in **power stations** and reaches our homes by a network of **power cables**.

   a)   In a gas-fired power station, gas is burned and its chemical energy is converted into heat energy.

      i)   Describe how this heat energy is then converted into electrical energy.

....

....

     ii)   If a power station is 38% efficient, how much energy is **wasted**
for every 1000 J of electrical energy **produced**?

....

....

   b)   Natural gas is a fossil fuel. Burning it releases carbon dioxide and contributes to climate change.

      i)   Suggest two alternative types of fuel which could be used to produce heat in power stations
without contributing to climate change.

.... and ....

     ii)   It is now possible to install photocells and wind turbines on the roof of a house. Explain why
few households in the UK could rely on these technologies for their electricity supply.

....

....

   c)   **i)**   Explain why electricity transmission cables are at very high voltages.

....

     ii)   What device is used to convert this high voltage into a voltage suitable for use in a house?

....

Q2   The diagram represents a **light wave** emitted from Cygnus A
— a galaxy about 700 million light years from Earth.

   a)   On the diagram, redraw the wave to show how it might
appear to us on Earth because the light is **red-shifted**.

   b)   Explain how red-shifts from distant and nearer galaxies
provide evidence for the Big Bang theory.

....

....

....

Module P2 — Living for the Future

Mixed Questions — Module P2

Q3   Jemima is using an **electric sander** which has a power rating of **360 W**.

a)   The electricity supply in Jemima's house is at 230 V. Calculate the **current** the sander draws.

....

b)   Jemima's electricity supplier charges **15.2p per kWh**. Jemima has the sander on for 45 minutes. How much does this cost (to the nearest penny)?

....

....

Q4   The table gives information about four different **radioisotopes**.

Source	Type of Radiation	Rate of Decay
radon-222	alpha	fast
technetium-99m	gamma	very fast
americium-241	alpha	very slow
cobalt-60	beta and gamma	slow

a)   Explain which of these sources you would use, and why, in:

i) a smoke detector

....

....

ii) a medical tracer

....

....

b)   Gamma radiation from cobalt-60 is used to test metal turbine blades for faults. What precautions should be taken by workers handling **cobalt-60**?

....

....

Q5   The diagram shows a **bicycle dynamo**. It is connected to a lamp (not shown).

a)   When the knob is rotated clockwise at a constant speed, the lamp lights up. Explain why.

....

....

....

knob to turn magnet

magnet

N   S

soft iron

coil

b)   What difference would you notice if the magnet was rotated:

i) anticlockwise? ....

ii) faster? ....

Module P2 — Living for the Future

Mixed Questions — Module P2

Q6   The Sun consists mainly of **hydrogen**. It also contains **helium**.

a)   In a few million years time, the Sun will contain **more helium** and **less hydrogen** than it does now. Explain why.

....

....

b)   The Sun is currently in its 'stable period'. What determines how long a star's stable period lasts?

....

c)   Will the Sun ever become a **black hole**? Explain your answer.

....

Q7   **Planets**, **moons**, **asteroids** and **comets** are all found in the Solar System.

a)   It is thought that the Moon was formed after the collision of another planet with the Earth. Give two pieces of evidence that support this theory.

....

....

....

b)   Explain what asteroids are and why they can pose a threat to life on Earth.

....

....

c)   Why do comets **speed up** as they get closer to the Sun?

....

Q8   Exploring space is expensive and dangerous.

a)   Name the eighth furthest planet from the Sun. ....

b)   Explain why it is unlikely that a manned mission will be sent to this planet in the near future.

....

....

....

....